REG

Make the most of your time:

BKB Verlag

VISIT THE CITY

A City Stroll

Regensburg in the Evening

Walhalla

3 Days in

St Emmeram

Historical Museum

Strolling and Shopping

Content

LEGEND

- ⌛ Duration of the tour
- ◆ Opening times/ departure times
- ▲ Transport stop
- ➤ see

Welcome to

© BKB Verlag
All rights reserved
1/11/16

Editor:
Dr. Brigitte Hintzen-Bohlen

Layout:
Elisa da Silva Filipe
Brandt GmbH, Bonn
www.druckerei-brandt.de

Translation into English:
John Sykes

English copy-editing:
Martin Simmonds

Printing:
Brandt GmbH, Bonn

ISBN 978-3-94091-4 77-4

BKB Verlag
Auerstrasse 4
50733 Köln
Telephone 0221/9521460
Fax   0221/5626446
www.bkb-verlag.de
mail@bkb-verlag.de

... one of the most beautiful cities in Germany, in the Oberpfalz region, with its Italian atmosphere and Bavarian way of life

... a UNESCO World Heritage site where the picturesque Old Town is an impressive example of a centre of medieval trade

... where kings and emperors once stayed, and German history was made

... where three rivers, the Danube, Naab and Regen, invite visitors to take long walks

... where the princes von Thurn und Taxis have their home

... a student city and a prosperous centre of business.

Regensburg

3 TIPS – HIGHLIGHTS – BEST OF

CITY HALL:
History is tangible in the Imperial Chamber.

CATHEDRAL:
See the oldest stained-glass windows in Europe in Bavaria's only Gothic cathedral.

STONE BRIDGE:
A masterpiece of medieval architecture

THURN UND TAXIS PALACE:
The princes' residence in a former Benedictine monastery is the largest inhabited palace in Europe.

SCOTTISH CHURCH OF ST JACOB:
The sculptural programme of the church entrance remains a riddle to this day.

DOMSPATZEN BOYS' CHOIR:
Listen to the world's oldest boys' choir on Sundays at 10 am in the cathedral.

OBERER WÖHRD:
From the wonderful, green meadow landscape of this island you have a view of the World Heritage Old Town.

BISMARCKPLATZ:
The people of Regensburg meet at the fountain between Café Anton and the theatre to enjoy the last of the evening sunshine.

About Regensburg

● The Old Town of Regensburg, with its patrician houses, towers, cathedral and Stone Bridge reflects the economic, political and religious developments of the high Middle Ages better than any other city in central Europe. The ensemble of "Regensburg Old Town with Stadtamhof" was therefore included on the UNESCO list of World Heritage sites in 2006. It is an outstanding example of an intact medieval city of the size that it had in the early 14th century.

● Many STREET NAMES in the Old Town are derived from medieval marketplaces or professions. Names of lanes like Drei-Mohren-Gasse (Three Moors), Silberne Fisch-Gasse (Silver Fish) and Fröhliche-Türken-Gasse (Happy Turk) hark back to inns that once stood here. The Tür family, for example, ran an inn called "Zum fröhlichen Mann" (The Happy Man).

● For meetings, lectures, exhibitions and other events the Grosser RUN-TIGERSAAL at Keplerstrasse 1 can be hired. This banqueting hall in an early Gothic patrician's house dating from the 13th and 14th centuries is impressive testimony to the prosperity and splendour of the Runtingers, Regensburg merchants.

● A broad GREEN BELT encloses the Old Town in a wide arc. It originated in the avenue which Prince Karl Anselm von Thurn und Taxis laid out in front of the old city wall between 1779 and 1781, and which was extended to make several large parks modelled on English landscape gardens.

● A memorial plaque in the cathedral commemorates the preacher DR JOHANN MAIER, who was accused of sabotage by the Nazis and executed on 24 April 1945.

On the previous day, he and others had spoken out in favour of surrendering the city peacefully to the Allies. This is one of the reasons why Regensburg was not destroyed in the war.

● House number 5 on Watmarkt was the home of the industrialist OSKAR SCHINDLER from November 1945 to May 1950. During the Second World War, Schindler saved the lives of approximately 1,200 Jews.

● Irmgard Schneeberger (1935-94), who became a famous German author under her nom de plume SANDRA PARETTI, grew up on Obere Wöhrd. Her novels *Rose and Sword* and *The Winter That Was a Summer* made her one of the most widely read writers of the German-speaking world.

● For the anniversary "750 Years of Municipal Rights", the City of Regensburg founded the BRÜCKENPREIS (Bridge Prize), which is awarded to persons who have made a special contribution to bridging political, national, scientific, social, cultural or religious differences, and have built bridges for the future. In 2016 the prize was awarded to Mikhail Gorbachev.

● Since 1998 the ARMIN-WOLF-ARENA has been home to the Buchbinder Legionäre, currently Germany's biggest baseball club. National and international matches are regularly held here, in Germany's largest baseball stadium.

● Regensburg is one of the leading ECONOMIC CENTRES in Germany, holding first place as the most dynamic location in the country and seventh place among 402 German districts and cities on the criterion of its prospects for the future.

For the historic lanterns in the Old Town, the company OSRAM developed energy-saving LEDs that halved power consumption and reduced CO_2 emissions by 30 tonnes.

A City Stroll

REICHSTAG IN REGENSBURG

When an empire consists of a host of large and small territories, as the Holy Roman Empire of the German Nation did, its administration is complex. Therefore its secular and spiritual representatives, the so-called estates of the empire (Reich), met under the leadership of the elected king at an assembly named the Reichstag in order to discuss matters of foreign relations, the economy and finances, and to pass laws. At first, Reichstag meetings were held in various places, but from 1594 their permanent seat was Regensburg. This was a central location on the Danube, close to Vienna, and open to both religious confessions, as the city had been Protestant since 1542 but was still the seat of a Catholic bishop and the site of many monasteries.

A CITY STROLL – TRINKET OF THE MIDDLE AGE

On a walk through the historic Old Town and Stadtamhof you will discover beautiful squares, old palaces and tall towers, learning about the secular and religious centre of the former Free Imperial City.

● HAIDPLATZ ①: This square is one of the most ancient in the Old Town and has a rich tradition. With fine residences around it, many cafés and restaurants, and the Baroque *Justitia Fountain* at its centre, it resembles an Italian piazza. Its unusual triangular shape goes back to a fork in the road in Roman times, and its name refers to a "heath" in front of the Roman camp. Used as a space for festivities and tournaments in the Middle Ages, the square is now home to many events such as the Bavarian Jazz Weekend and craft markets.

● NEUE WAAG ②: As the name ("new scales") suggests, from 1441 the municipal weighing station was situated in this red patrician palace with its tower on the eastern side. It was also the site of the tavern room, where members of the city council took a drink during breaks in meetings to continue their discus-

sions informally. The building became famous during the Colloquy of Regensburg in 1541, in which Phillip Melanchthon and Leonhard von Eck unsuccessfully tried to reconcile the Protestant and Roman Catholic confessions. The mural painting in the arcaded courtyard refers to this. To the south is the *Arch* ③, also a townhouse, dating from the 13th century, with beautiful Gothic windows. It has the shape of the bows of a ship, and is occupied by a hotel today.

● ZUM GOLDENEN KREUZ ④: The building that dominates Haidplatz, the Golden Cross, is an early Gothic patrician fortified house with a seven-storey tower. Since the 16th century it has accommodated many princes, kings and emperors. In this fine residence, rulers from King Ludwig I of Bavaria to Wilhelm I of Prussia, later German emperor, and Emperor Franz Josef I of Austria have stayed.

● THON-DITTMER-PALAIS ⑤: In the classical palace next door, converted by the Thon-Dittmer family of merchants to make two medieval buildings into a single ensemble with four wings, do not fail to take a look at the atmospheric Renaissance-style arcaded courtyard. In summer it is used as a venue for many cultural events. Above the arch of the gate, a life-size statue of a woman with an hour-glass admonishes the beholder as follows: "The sand has run out of the glass, mark that the time has come to die", possibly referring to the old man on the relief of the Gothic bay window, who wants to regain his youth through the love of a young girl.

DOLLINGER'S BATTLE AGAINST CRACO THE GIANT

The most famous battle fought on Haidplatz, according to Regensburg legend, took place around the year 930: while King Heinrich I and his retinue were staying in Regensburg, the heathen knight Craco scorned the royal knights and challenged them to a duel. As the huge Craco was thought to be invincible and his shield bearing a devil struck fear into every heart, no one dared take up the challenge. Only the citizen Hans Dollinger, who was in prison, declared he would fight Craco if he was released in return. At the tomb of Saint Erhard in the Lower Minster he prayed for victory and was advised to set up a cross at the place of battle. After Craco had succeeded twice in unsaddling Dollinger, the brave citizen was given a cross by the king, and defeated his adversary at the third attempt.

IDIOMS FROM THE REICHSTAG

Several common expressions in the German language derive from the assemblies in Regensburg. "To push something onto a long bench" (to delay or postpone) derives from the lengthy deliberations of the Reich estates, who sat on long benches. "To throw money out of the window" refers to the custom that the emperor tossed coins into the crowds from the loggia. To make decisions "at a green table" (in a committee/from an armchair, without practical guidance) comes from the round table in the building, a secret chamber of the prince electors, which was covered in a green cloth. A "Katzentisch" (literally "cat's table", a corruption of "Ketzertisch", meaning "heretics' table") is not the top table. The expression was used by Catholic bishops for the table at which the Protestant prince bishops of Osnabrück and Lübeck sat.

● **RATHAUS ⑥**: In the Rathaus (city hall), European history was made: the precursors of the German and European parliaments met here! For centuries assemblies of the Holy Roman Empire and later delegations of the Perpetual Diet of Regensburg met here.

Until the 19th century the tower of the Rathaus was the tallest building of the city, and thus a visible sign of its centre. The dukes ruled from their palace on the old Kornmarkt, but when Regensburg became a Free Imperial City in 1245, a city hall was called for. Its citizens needed a building to represent their status, as from this time onwards they were directly subject to the emperor and could run their own affairs. The four-winged Rathaus with its eight-storey tower dates from this period, and was extended up to the 18th century to make it a larger complex.

The wing that now houses the tourist information office dates from the mid-14th century. On the lower floor traders sold their wares and courts of law met, while on the upper floor, behind the row of windows and Gothic loggia, lay the banqueting hall, a historic venue known as the Reichssaal. From 1594 all meetings of the Reichstag, and from 1663 for 143 years the Perpetual Diet, were held here. For insights into medieval law and order, go down to the cellars to see the original dungeons and the Fragstatt, the place of interrogation where prisoners were tortured to gain confessions.

THE PERPETUAL DIET

When the Reichstag of 1663 failed to reach agreement and could not be dissolved, it became a permanent institution that played its part in European politics until the abolition of the Holy Roman Empire in 1806. Understandably the ruling princes could not be present at all times, so they were represented by delegates.

The office of emperor's representative, the "principal commissar", was held from 1748 by the princes of Thurn und Taxis (➤ p. 13). For Regensburg, where the age of economic prosperity had ended in the 15th century, this development was an important boost. Baroque magnificence came to the city, as the delegates ("Gesandte") from Germany

and other parts of Europe brought courtiers and servants, spent money, hired and adorned fine residences, and held opulent festivities, balls, concerts and theatre performances. Testimony to these times can still be seen in the Gesandtenstrasse and delegation buildings such as the Ingolstetterhaus, Löschenkohlpalais and Thon-Dittmer-Palais.

TOWERS AS SYMBOLS OF POWER

The Romanesque and Gothic buildings of the Old Town are impressive testament to the prosperity of Regensburg in the Middle Ages. With its skyline formed from many towers of churches and the city wall, as well as those of patrician families, the city resembles a "medieval New York". The northernmost city on the Danube, Regensburg became wealthy as a junction of important routes for long-distance trade that stretched as far as the Bosphorus and even India. As a status symbol to show their economic and political power, rich merchants built houses with stone towers. The richer the family, the higher the tower that they built. In some periods about 60 towers looked down on the roofs of the city. Architecturally these towers, known as Geschlechtertürme (dynastic towers), are modelled on those in northern Italy. Despite their fortified appearance, with slits for shooting and crenellations, they primarily served the purpose of ostentation.

Adjoining to the right is the Staircase Building with its fine Gothic entrance, on which two warlike figures above the two coats of arms express the military strength of the city. On the left medieval measurements, a foot, a fathom and an ell, which were considered symbols of the city's wealth as they were above average in length, are marked on the wall. The Baroque wing facing Kohlenmarkt is from the period of the Perpetual Diet.

● ALTER KOHLENMARKT ⑦: When you stroll across the wide marketplace of the early medieval

3 TIP Don't fail to book a tour of the historic rooms of the Rathaus, called the Reichstagsmuseum. It is truly fascinating! Tickets are available right next to the entrance in the tourist information office.
Rathausplatz 1, tour: 10am, 11.30am, 1.30pm, 3pm, 3.30pm (Nov, March), 10am, 11.30am, 1.30pm, 3.30pm (Jan-Feb), every half hour from 9.30am to 12 noon, 1.30-4pm (Apr-Oct); tour in English: 2pm (Nov-March), 3pm (Apr-Oct)

town with its numerous cafés, you are at the heart of the old merchants' quarter. Luxury goods of all kinds were traded in the narrow streets and on the squares and marketplaces. The magnificent patrician houses demonstrate the wealth of the

DON JUAN DE AUSTRIA

Why does Regensburg commemorate, with a relief portrait on the Goldenes Kreuz and a bronze statue on Zieroldsplatz next to the city hall, the man who gained a brilliant victory for the Holy League over the Ottoman fleet in 1571 at the battle of Lepanto? Because this famous military commander was the child of a liaison

between Emperor Charles V and Barbara Blomberg, the daughter of a burgher of Regensburg, during the Reichstag of 1546! After the birth, the monarch immediately gave recognition to his son and sent him to foster parents in Spain at the age of three. There he grew up without knowing his true family background. It was only after the death of the emperor that his successor, complying with Charles V's last will and testament, brought his half-brother to the royal court.

merchants. At Wahlenstrasse no. 16 stands the tallest domestic tower north of the Alps, the Goldener Turm. This *Golden Tower* ⑧, with its nine storeys and height of 50 metres, dates to around 1260 and was part of a fortified townhouse with four wings. It takes its name from an inn that was later here, and is now student accommodation.

Have a break

In Germany's oldest coffeehouse, also the court supplier for the princes of Thurn und Taxis, in the **Café Prinzess** directly opposite, you can digest the history with your coffee and cake. *Rathausplatz 2* ◆ *Mon-Sat 9am-6.30pm, Sun 10am-6.30pm, www.cafe-prinzess.de*

Have a break 🍴2

With its Renaissance arcades, fountain of the goose-preacher, and view of the cathedral and Eselsturm (➤ p. 19), the beer garden in the courtyard of the **Bischofshof** hotel is an idyllic spot.

Krauterermarkt 3
◆ *10am-midnight*

THE GOOSE SERMON

A well-known fable is the story of the false preacher. As the fox did not succeed in catching any of the quick geese, he disguised himself as a priest and preached to the animals until they had all fallen asleep. Then

● WATMARKT: In the lane called Watmarkt ("Wat" is an old word meaning "robe"), directly on the right behind Alter Kohlenmarkt, fine cloth was once traded. With all its towers and oriels it still conveys an impression of how the city looked in the Middle Ages. One of the most splendid patrician towers is the seven-storey *Baumburger Turm* ⑨ with its round-arched loggia and three-part, early Gothic groups of windows at number 4. It was built in about 1270 by the Ingolstetter family. The ground floor, today a restaurant, was once occupied by the house chapel.

● GOLIATHHAUS ⑩: A short detour into Brückstrasse is a must, because from here you have a good view of the Gothic "Goliath house". It is the largest fortified house in Regensburg, a classic ensemble with a powerful tower and a residential wing crowned by strong battlements. Its façade dating from about 1563 is adorned by the scene of David's fight against Goliath, but this fresco did not give the building its name. The origin was probably the pre-

they were at his mercy. This tale is wonderfully depicted on the Goose-Preacher Fountain by Joseph Michael Neustifter (1980) in the lovely courtyard of the Bischofshof. On the rear side, the preacher is revealed in his true form!

vious structure on the site, an inn of the "Goliards", as wandering theology students called themselves, after their patron Goliath.

Goliathstraße 4

● BISCHOFSHOF ⑪: The hotel on the corner of Krauterermarkt (the market-place where herbs were sold) refers with its name ("bishop's court") to the former function of this four-wing building, which goes back to the 12th century. Emperors and kings stayed here for centuries, until the bishops moved out in 1825 to Niedermünster, a convent for noble ladies. In 1910 the building was converted into a hotel.

Krauterermarkt 3,
www.hotel-bischofshof.de

● PORTA PRAETORIA ⑫: This gate, which was partially built into the Bischofshof and was therefore not plundered as a source of stone, leads back to the Roman history of Regensburg. Only one tower and an arch remain of what was originally a two-storey double gate flanked by two semi-circular projecting towers made from massive stone blocks. It was the north gate, one of four entrances to the *Castra Regina* military camp (➤ p. 42). Next to the Porta Nigra in Trier, it is the only surviving Roman gateway in Germany.

Unter den Schwibbögen 2
◆ closed for restoration

● DOMPLATZ ⑬: The L-shaped cathedral square was formed from two different open spaces. The density of the buildings underlines once again the dominance of the merchants in relation to the bishop, who ruled the roost only in his own, confined cathedral precinct after 1245 and was not able to build an imposing avenue in order to enter the cathedral in pomp.

The north side of Domplatz is taken up by the Baroque façade of St Johann, a collegiate church and once the baptistery of the Romanesque cathedral. This church was moved and reconstructed when the cathedral was newly built. Opposite is the *Adlerbrunnen* (Eagle Fountain), with the figure of an eagle, an imperial symbol, perched on an orb and looking towards the cathedral.

● HAUS HEUPORT ⑭: Among the buildings on the west side of Domplatz, the house with a beautiful Gothic façade catches the eye. Windows in the Venetian Gothic style – behind which lies a large banqueting hall – rise above the entrance to the courtyard of this big patrician residence. It was built by Carl Kratzer († 1355), who had an important position in the city as head of the guild of merchants engaged in long-distance trade. The name of the building derives from the small Heutor (Hay Gate), which led to the adjoining Jewish quarter in the Middle Ages (➤ p.40).

● DOM ST. PETER ⑮

With towers that can be seen from afar, the cathedral (Dom) is a landmark of the city that contains an impressive number of works of art, including colourful windows that are among the oldest examples of stained glass in Europe. It is home to the Regensburger Domspatzen boys' choir and also the only Gothic cathedral in Bavaria.

Before entering the church, take a look at the imposing west façade, which has two conspicuous elements: the discrepancy between the two towers, which is a sign of the long construction period, and the differences of colour, which is a consequence of the use of various building materials including, white limestone and green sandstone. Take some time to admire the opulent sculptural decoration, which conveys an idea of the religious beliefs of the Middle Ages. Among its depictions is the Freeing of St Peter in the arch above the south doorway, on which an angel raises

A CATHEDRAL RECORD-BREAKER

The impressive "swallow's-nest organ" on the north wall of the transept, over 18 metres high, nearly 8 metres wide and weighing almost 37 tonnes, is suspended from four steel cables and has more than 80 stops with a total of 5871 pipes, divided between four manuals and the pedals. This makes the instrument, built in 2009 by the Austrian company Rieger, the world's largest suspended organ. It can be played from two different consoles, the main one being accessed via a concealed lift.

3 | TIP At twelve o'clock from Monday to Friday (from the Tuesday after Easter until 31 October) the cathedral invites all visitors to spend a quarter hour at midday in contemplation, to the sound of organ music. *domplatz-5. de/domplatz-5/12-uhr-mittags*

the prison tower and takes out the patron saint of the cathedral. A document of those times is the Judensau (an image showing Jews sucking at the teats of a sow) on the south of the nave, one of many such insulting representations of Jews made in medieval times.

An unusual feature is the *Eselsturm* (Donkey Tower) on the north transept, which is best viewed from the courtyard of the *Bischofshof*. It was part of the Romanesque predecessor of the cathedral and was used for raising building materials to its upper parts.

Those who enter the interior with its nave and two aisles are surprised at first by the darkness. Little light penetrates the original stained-glass windows dating from the 13th and 14th centuries. This creates a spatial impression like that of the Middle Ages. If you take the trouble, it is possible to read, like believers of old, the numerous stories that are told by the small, colourful pieces of glass that make up the windows.

MORE THAN 600 YEARS IN THE MAKING

When Saint Boniface founded the diocese of Regensburg in the year 739, the foundation stone was soon laid for the first basilica. After several alterations and rebuildings, in 1260 the construction of today's cathedral in the Gothic style began, a few metres away from the previous church. Thanks to generous donations by rich merchants, building work proceeded well in the following two centuries until the economic decline of Regensburg led to ever more frequent interruptions in construction, and work had to be stopped altogether in 1520. At this time the cathedral was finished apart from the vaulting over the crossing and the upper parts of the west towers. It was not until the reign of King Ludwig I that building recommenced, and was completed in 1872. In the course of this work, almost all the Baroque additions were removed to give the cathedral a "Gothic" appearance again.

DIOZESANMUSEUM

Many works of art can be admired inside the cathedral. The blond-haired Laughing Angel from the larger than life-size Annunciation on the west piers of the crossing (by the Erminold Master, c. 1280) is a famous example of Gothic sculpture. In the niches to the left and right of the main entrance, note two small figures of demons, popularly known as the devil and his grandmother. In fact their purpose is to keep evil spirits away from the church. The magnificent silver high altar made by silversmiths from Augsburg was formed over a period of almost 100 years from individual donations by bishops and cathedral canons (1695-1785). The five richly decorated Gothic altars with canopies in the two aisles are another rarity.

Domplatz 5 ♦ 6.30am-6pm (Apr-May, Oct), 6.30am-7pm (June-Sept) 6.30am-5pm (Nov-March), www.bistum-regensburg.de/bistum/dom-st-peter/

For tours, refer to the Catholic information and visitor centre DOMPLATZ 5: domplatz-5.de

● DOMSCHATZMUSEUM ⑯: The importance of Regensburg as a centre of goldsmith work up to the 18th century is shown by the exhibition in the **Domschatzmuseum**. It occupies the former bishop's residence and is accessed via the north transept.

DOMSPATZEN BOYS' CHOIR

The Regensburger Domspatzen ("Cathedral Sparrows") are one of the oldest and most famous boys' choirs in the world. Their origins lie in the foundation of a cathedral school by Bishop Wolfgang in the year 975. Even in those days, the pupils had the task of accompanying the liturgy of cathedral services. The international reputation of the Domspatzen, consisting only of boys and young men, is owed to Dr Theobald Schrems. In his 40 years as master of cathedral music, until 1963, he continually extended the activities of the choir, including tours abroad – though his role during the years of Nazi rule has been questioned. Then Georg Ratzinger, the brother of Pope Benedict XVI, conducted the choir for 30 years. Since 1994 Roland Büchner has been the musical director. Under his leadership Regensburg's singing ambassadors have performed further great choral works and undertaken many tours to other countries *(www.domspatzen.de)*

Krauterermarkt 3 ♦ Tue-Sat 11am-5pm, Sun 12pm-5pm (Apr-Nov), Fri-Sat 11am-5pm, Sun 12pm-5pm (Dec-Mar)

www.bistum-regensburg.de/ bistum/dom-st-peter/der-regens-burger-domschatz/

● CATHEDRAL CLOISTER ⑰:
Following restoration that will probably last until 2020, it will be possible to visit the Romanesque double cloister again. Its middle part was used for the burial of high-ranking persons. The 12th-century Allerheiligenkapelle (All Saints' Chapel) with paintings of the All Saints Mass is an architectural gem. It was built with a central plan by Bishop Hartwig II of Spanheim to serve as a mausoleum. He was the first bishop of Regensburg who was not buried in St Emmeram's monastery.

(domplatz-5.de)

3 **TIP** You can hear the Domspatzen boys' choir every Sunday at 10am in the cathedral, when they sing during the main service (except in the school holidays).

● ST. ULRICH/ DIÖZESAN-MUSEUM ⑱: In 2018 a fascinating museum in one of the oldest Gothic buildings in Germany will reopen. Erected as the chapel for the ducal palace during the remodelling of the duke's court between 1220 and 1230, the building became the cathedral's parish church a decade later. With its massive flying buttresses on the outside, this basilica with double aisles has a fortified appearance. The superb rose window above the main west doorway is unique in Regensburg, and there are precious remains of frescoes, part of the original wall paintings, inside the church.

Domplatz2
www.bistumsmuseen-regensburg. de/museum-st-ulrich.html

CARMELITE CHURCH OF ST JOSEPH ㉓

The church on the east side of Alter Kornmarkt reminds many visitors of Santa Maria della Scala in Rome. Indeed, this two-storey Baroque façade with large volutes flanking the upper part is modelled on the mother church of the Barefoot Carmelites in Rome. The monastery is known for its Karmelitengeist liqueur, made from pure natural spices and herbs, which is said to be a good remedy for colds, and is on sale next to the church.

Alter Kornmarkt 7
www.karmelitenkloster-stjoseph.de

● ALTER KORNMARKT ⑲: This square, named in the days when it was a marketplace for trading grain, was the area controlled by the dukes until Regensburg was made a Free Imperial City in 1245, and was therefore also next to the centre of clerical power. Here in the 6th century the Bavarian ducal dynasty, the Agilolfings, built a palace that was then taken over by the Carolingian monarchs and became a royal residence. Under Ludwig the German (825-876) it was extended to become a magnificent complex, in use until Regensburg became a Free Imperial City.

● ROMAN TOWER AND BISHOP'S COURT ⑳: The strong, square tower with a base of massive granite blocks was part of the ducal residence. It is known as the Römerturm (Roman Tower), and is connected by an arch to the duke's palace, which once had four wings. The arch now leads to the only remaining part of the residence, the east wing (c. 1220) with the large *Herzogssaal* (Ducal Chamber) on the upper floor, which is now used for events *(herzogssaal.com)*

● OLD CHAPEL ㉑: On the south side of the square is the Alte Kapelle, a palace chapel on the site of a first church from the time of the Roman emperor Constantine the Great, and one of the oldest churches in the city. Today's broad building with a free-standing bell tower was built in about 1002 by the later Emperor Heinrich II, altered several times and extended by the addition of the Gothic choir. This collegiate church dedicated to Our Lady of the Old Chapel is famous for its unique Rococo interior, which was installed for the 750th anniversary of the foundation. A programme of frescoes and sculptures showing scenes from the life of Heinrich II and his wife Kunigunde form a wonderful symbiosis with the architecture, stucco work and ornaments.

In the Gnadenkapelle (Votive Chapel) is a famous painting, the *Gnadenbild*, a depiction of the Virgin Mary with the Christ Child that, according to legend, was painted by St Luke the Evangelist. It was a gift from Pope Benedict VIII to Emperor Heinrich II on the occasion of his coronation in 1014, as depicted on the ceiling paintings in the nave. Another notable item is the modern Pope Benedict Organ, which was consecrated by Benedict XVI in person in 2006.

▲ *Alter Kornmarkt, tours 11am on the last Tuesday in the month (May-Oct), www.alte-kapelle.de*

● NIEDERMÜNSTER ㉒: Two Romanesque towers and a strongly built vestibule show the way to what is today the cathedral parish church, in which the peripatetic bishop St Erhard is buried. This basilica, with a nave separated from its two aisles by pillars, dates from the mid-12th century and was later remodelled in Baroque style. The complex of buildings served for a long time as a collegiate institution for unmarried or widowed noblewomen, who were, however, allowed to leave and marry at any time. The eye-catching feature inside is the three-part Gothic canopy in the north aisle above the tomb of St Erhard. On the right is a reliquary shrine containing the top of the saint's skull in a silver receptacle; his effigy in stone lies beneath.

▲ *Niedermünstergasse,* ◆ *8am-6pm Document Niedermünster: www.document-niedermuenster.de, guided tour: Sun+Mon 3.30 pm*

SALT – WHITE GOLD

Salt has always been a coveted item of trade. Salt roads are the oldest commercial routes in Europe. The possession of salt and control of its trade made it possible to raise salt taxes, which meant wealth and power. For Regensburg this economic activity was highly significant. The salt came up the Danube via Passau from deposits in Reichenhall, and was distributed to other places from the city. Initially trading was in the hands of salt lords, but in the 16th century the city government took control. The dukes of Bavaria tried to evade the customs duties that Regensburg, as a Free Imperial City, was allowed to impose on ships by building their own salt store, the Andreas-Stadel in Stadtamhof, and forcibly hauling the salt ships beneath the northern Stone Bridge. Regensburg could not stand by and let this happen: the city employed the shipper Hanns Heygl to cut the ropes of the Bavarian salt ships with an axe, so that they were carried away by the current and had to reload.

● SALZSTADEL/VISITOR CENTRE ㉔: The large warehouse building with its tall, five-storey pitched roof dating from the early 17th century impressively emphasises Regensburg's former importance as a trading city. Today the Salzstadel is a visitor centre: since the Old Town and Stadtamhof with their more than 1,000 protected buildings became a UNESCO World Heritage site in 2006, an exhibition here has illuminated the 2,000-year history of Regensburg.

Weiße-Lamm-Gasse 1 ◆ *10am-7pm*
www.regensburg.de/welterbe/besucherzentrum

● STONE BRIDGE ㉕: A second emblem of the city is the Steinerne Brücke, the bridge that was built by the merchants in 1135 to promote economic growth. In only eleven years, a technical and artistic masterpiece was constructed. It spanned the Danube with 16 barrel arches (today 15) and a length of 336 metres, serving as a model for many other stone bridges. A typical characteristic of such medieval bridges are the massive stone islands around the piers, to protect the bridge from erosion by water. Their width acts as a dam, holding back the water upstream and causing a swirling current, the reason why many mills were established here to take advantage of the water power.

For centuries the Stone Bridge was the only permanent crossing of the Danube between Ulm and Vienna, and therefore an important traffic node. Three watchtowers, of which only the south bridge tower

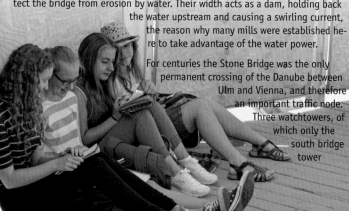

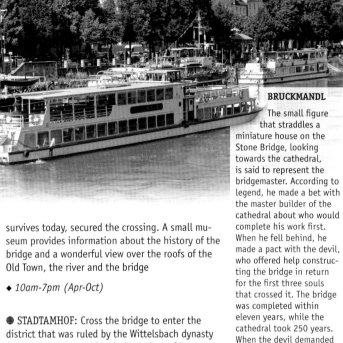

BRUCKMANDL

The small figure that straddles a miniature house on the Stone Bridge, looking towards the cathedral, is said to represent the bridgemaster. According to legend, he made a bet with the master builder of the cathedral about who would complete his work first. When he fell behind, he made a pact with the devil, who offered help constructing the bridge in return for the first three souls that crossed it. The bridge was completed within eleven years, while the cathedral took 250 years. When the devil demanded his reward, the bridgemaster drove two cocks and a dog across the bridge. The devil was so angry at being tricked in this way, that he began to destroy the bridge. However, it was too solidly built, and today only a slight bend remains.

survives today, secured the crossing. A small museum provides information about the history of the bridge and a wonderful view over the roofs of the Old Town, the river and the bridge

◆ *10am-7pm (Apr-Oct)*

● STADTAMHOF: Cross the bridge to enter the district that was ruled by the Wittelsbach dynasty for centuries. It was thus independent of Regensburg – enemy territory, as it were. For this reason the settlement benefited from the trade route over the Stone Bridge, but was always the first target for attack in times of war, during which it was completely destroyed several times. Since 1924 this former "town at the court near Regensburg", "Stat am Hof bay Regensburg", has been part of the city.

Have a break

In the **Spitalgarten**, one of the pleasantest beer gardens on the north arm of the Danube, with a view of the Stone Bridge and the city, try the excellent beers while sitting under centuries-old chestnut trees.
St.-Katharinen-Platz 1 ◆ 9am-midnight, www.garten.spital.de

DANUBE ISLAND

When you cross the Stone Bridge, elongated, fish-shaped islands with extensive parkland and water meadows on both sides catch the eye. This kind of island in the river is called a Wöhrd. For the locals, they are places to spend time in a beer garden, have a barbecue, sunbathe or simply relax. On the upper or *Obere Wöhrd* ㉘ to the left of the bridge, where you can still see fishermen's and boatmen's houses as well as summer villas on Badstrasse and Lieblstrasse, the recreational facilities include a park and a pool, the Wöhrdbad. The lower island, *Untere Wöhrd* ㉙, where boatmen, artisans and rafters lived, is linked to the Old Town by the *Iron Bridge*.

At the end the bridge, once the site of the bridge tower, now a scene of small cafés and restaurants, you reach Am Brückenbasar. In summer it feels like Italy here! On the left is the St Katharinenspital, an enclave of the Free Imperial City across the river, and the most important welfare institution of Regensburg in past times. To give the sick inmates a bedtime drink, a brewery was founded, the Spitalbrauerei, which now looks back on an 800-year history.

◆ *tours: tel. 0941/83006187, www.spital.de*

Next to the Hochschule für Katholische Kirchenmusik und Musikpädagogik (College for Catholic Church Music and Music Teaching) in the buildings of the Augustinian monastery, the *Church of St Mang* ㉖ is worth a look for its opulent Rococo decoration. Walk along the idyllic lane past the *Andreasstadel* ㉗, the Bavarian dukes' salt store, now used as a hotel, cinema, theatre and house of artists, then across the *Eiserne Brücke* (Iron Bridge) back to the Old Town.

Regensburg in the Evening

REGENSBURG
IN THE EVENING

The lights don't go out in the evening in Regensburg. People flock to the Old Town, not only when the weather is warm. And whatever you enjoy – somewhere trendy, a rustic pub, a beer garden, a cool lounge or cocktail bar, a club for dancing, a big disco or live music – you will find something to suit your taste.

For going out in Regensburg there are lots of alternatives in and around the Old Town, along the Danube and near the Stone Bridge. This district feels as if it must be the area with the biggest concentration of pubs in Germany, and the party goes on into the early hours of the morning. People are on the move everywhere, in the streets and narrow alleys, on numerous open squares, sitting together for a meal or meeting for a beer or glass of wine.

A popular rendezvous on warm summer nights is the fountain on **Bismarckplatz**, where the locals meet their friends, bask in the last rays of sunshine and make their plans for the evening. The *Neue Filmbühne* cinema and *Café Anton* on Bismarckplatz or other small places close by in Drei-Mohren-Strasse also make a wonderful start to a night out. From here you can simply drift along, as the bars and pubs are lined up one after another.

The **Jahn Island** and **Obere Wöhrd** are also favourite places for young people to meet in summer. Next to them, the *Alte Linde* beer garden has a superb view of the Old Town by night. If you continue across the Stone Bridge, the little square Am **Brückenbasar** in Stadtamhof is reminiscent of an Italian piazza. In the two L-shaped buildings flanking it, cafés and restaurants with their outdoor seating are inviting places to linger. Directly adjoining is the *Spitalgarten* with its brewhouse pub and a large beer garden.

For those who love to dance, the *Petersweg-Parkhaus* is the location of choice. With its legendary *Suite15*, its temple of techno, Club *Schimmerlos*, Disco *Beats* and the fashionable *Gatsby*, it has no fewer than four clubs for dancing and partying. Another option in the evening is a performance of theatre or music.

REGENSBURG CALENDAR

MARCH

International Thurn und Taxis Festival of cabaret: *www.alte-maelzerei.de*

remove dash (short film): *www.kurzfilmwoche.de*

APRIL

City hall concerts : *www.regensburg.de*

MAY

Maidult (fair): www.regensburg.de/dult

Regensburg Marathon: *www.regensburg-marathon.de*

JUNE

City festival: *stadtmaus.de*

Garden show: *www.thurnundtaxisgartenschau.de*

Dialect festival: *www.mundartfestival-regensburg.de*

Museum serenades: *www.museums-serenaden.de*

Early music: *www.tagealtermusik-regensburg.de*

JULY

Bavarian Jazz Weekend: *bayerisches-jazzweekend.de*

Jahn Island festival: *jahninselfest.de*

Klangfarben Festival – cultures of the world: *www.klangfarben.org/festival*

Regensburger Spectaculum: *stadtmaus.de/regensburger-spectaculum.html*

Palace festival: *www.schlossfestspiele-regensburg.de/*

WeinMusikFest: *www.regensburg.de*

AUGUST

Palazzo-Festival: *www.regensburg.de*

Regensburg Triathlon: *www.tristar-regensburg.de/triathlon*

Salve Abusina: *stadtmaus.de*

Silent movie week: *www.filmgalerie.de*

SEPTEMBER

Autumn fair: *www.regensburg.de/dult*

Regensburg Kulturpflaster (street entertainers): *www.mischkultur.org*

Stadtamhof wine festival: *www.regensburg.de*

NOVEMBER

Regensburg dance festival: *www.regensburger-tanztage.de*

DECEMBER

Advent market in the Katharinenspital: *stadtmaus.de*

Christmas market on Neupfarrplatz: *www.regensburg.de/christkindlmarkt*

Lucrezia-Markt: *www.lucrezia-markt.de*

Romantic Christmas market at Schloss Thurn und Taxis: *www.romantischer-weihnachtsmarkt-thurnundtaxis.de*

DON'T MARRY ACROSS THE DANUBE

... was the motto for centuries on both sides of the river. The existence side by side of the Free Imperial City of Regensburg and the district of Stadtamhof, belonging to the Duchy of Bavaria, led to many conflicts. The burghers of Regensburg, as proud citizens of the Holy Roman Empire, did not want to mix with the subjects of Bavarian dukes – and this attitude continued, long after Regensburg had lost its status as a Free Imperial City. To see how serious the rivalry was, take a look at the coat of arms of Stadtamhof, which bears three keys of St Peter – one more than the arms of the city of Regensburg.

The *Theater am Bismarkplatz* stages musicals, drama, dance, youth theatre and concerts. Go to the *Stadttheater* for varied offerings including cabaret, and to the *Turmtheater* for comedy, cabaret and improvised theatre. Jazz lovers go to the *jazz club Leerer Beutel* in the Städtische Galerie, and concerts in various genres are on the programme at the *Alte Mälzerei* arts centre. All year round there are diverse special events, some of them on an annual basis, for example the *Tage Alter Musik* (early music), the *Bavarian Jazz-Weekend*, the *Thurn und Taxis Schlossfestspiele* (palace festival) and the *Regensburger Tanztage* for dance.

St Emmeram

A City Stroll

Regensburg in the Evening

Walhalla

3 Days in

Historical Museum

St Emmeram

Strolling and Shopping

EMMERAM OF REGENSBURG

St Emmeram is revered in Regensburg as the first bishop of the city and its patron saint. Born in the 7th century in Poitiers in Aquitaine, during his missionary journeys Emmeram came to the court of the Bavarian duke and worked to spread the Christian faith in Regensburg. When Uta, the unmarried daughter of Duke Theodor, became pregnant, Emmeram advised her to say that he was the father in order to save her from punishment. When Emmeram then set off on a planned pilgrimage to Rome, his departure was interpreted as flight. Uta's brother Lantpert intercepted the bishop near Munich on 22 September 652 and tortured him to death. Immediately after this martyrdom, it rained for 40 days. Having learned the truth of the matter, Duke Theodor transferred the saint's corpse to Regensburg and ceremonionsly buried it there. Since 752 the bones have rested in the crypt of the church that is dedicated to Emmeram.

SAINTS AND PRINCES – ST EMMERAM

A visit to the former Benedictine monastery is a trip back in time to various historical periods, a chance to see the apartments of a princely family, to learn about "Scots" in Regensburg and to look out over the roofs of the city.

● ST EMMERAM ㉚: Visible from a distance, a free-standing bell tower looms over Emmeramsplatz and marks the location of a former Benedictine abbey that is one of the oldest in Bavaria. It originated at the grave of the martyr St Emmeram, where Benedictines established their monastery.

Through a wall with a Gothic double portal and painted blind arcades you enter the atrium of the church. This was once a cemetery, as shown by the large number of tombstones and memorials, including an epitaph for Aventinus, the first Bavarian historian. Note an unusual architectural feature, the 12th-century church of St Rupert, directly adjoining. It was once the parish church for the monastery, and is entered through the left-hand door in the Romanesque vestibule. Before you enter the basilica through the other door, don't miss the three medieval stone reliefs depicting Jesus Christ between St Emmeram and St Dionysius. It is one of the oldest remaining sculptural works in south Germany.

Next, you will think you have taken a leap through time: beyond the dark vestibule lies a bright, highly colourful, playfully Baroque interior that the brothers Cosmas Damian and Egid Quirin Asam adorned with impressive stucco work and with murals and ceiling paintings. The paintings between the larger than life-size statues of emperors and Benedictines represent scenes from the life of St Emmeram, the fresco above the chancel depicts the missionary activities of the Benedictines, and the one in the nave the martyrdom of Regensburg

Christians. The painting above the high altar (by Joachim Sandrart, 1666) is dedicated to the martyrdom of St Emmeram. Beneath it is the tomb of the saint, surrounded by a circular crypt dating from the 8th century. Pass beneath the organ gallery to enter the west transept. Here the Romanesque crypt holds the mortal remains of Bishop Wolfgang of Regensburg.

Emmeramsplatz 3,

▲ *Emmeramsplatz,*

◆ *Mon-Thu 10am-4pm, Fri + Sun 12 noon-4pm, Sat 9am-4pm (winter), Mon-Thu 10am-6pm, Fri + Sun 12 noon-6pm, Sat 9am-5pm (summer), www.st-emmeram-regensburg.de*

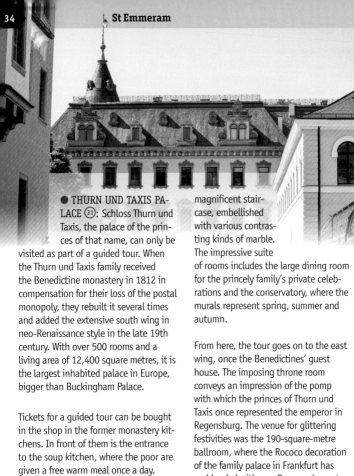

● THURN UND TAXIS PALACE ㉛: Schloss Thurn und Taxis, the palace of the princes of that name, can only be visited as part of a guided tour. When the Thurn und Taxis family received the Benedictine monastery in 1812 in compensation for their loss of the postal monopoly, they rebuilt it several times and added the extensive south wing in neo-Renaissance style in the late 19th century. With over 500 rooms and a living area of 12,400 square metres, it is the largest inhabited palace in Europe, bigger than Buckingham Palace.

Tickets for a guided tour can be bought in the shop in the former monastery kitchens. In front of them is the entrance to the soup kitchen, where the poor are given a free warm meal once a day.

Tours start at the Kurfürstenbrunnen (Prince Electors' Fountain) in the palace courtyard, which is the backdrop for the palace festival in summer and for the Christmas market. The south wing, where the state rooms of the princely residence are situated, is reached via a magnificent staircase, embellished with various contrasting kinds of marble. The impressive suite of rooms includes the large dining room for the princely family's private celebrations and the conservatory, where the murals represent spring, summer and autumn.

From here, the tour goes on to the east wing, once the Benedictines' guest house. The imposing throne room conveys an impression of the pomp with which the princes of Thurn und Taxis once represented the emperor in Regensburg. The venue for glittering festivities was the 190-square-metre ballroom, where the Rococo decoration of the family palace in Frankfurt has blended with neo-Rococo elements to form intoxicating festive architecture. Take a look at the circular upper windows, which show how two storeys of the monastery buildings were combined to make a space with a height of seven metres. During the palace festival (Schlossfestspiele), the orchestra plays here. The singers have to

take their cue by looking at the video screen on which the performance is relayed to the courtyard. The four-sided corner tower, crowned by a prince's hat, is the palace chapel in the style of the Venetian Renaissance. Here ,the Princess of Thurn und Taxis holds her private services, and the family children are baptised.

THURN UND TAXIS

The famous aristocratic dynasty of Thurn und Taxis was successful in business from the very beginning. They originally came from Lombardy, where the Tasso family (Italian for "badger") established an efficient courier system between the major Italian cities from 1290 onwards. When the later Emperor Maximilian I commissioned them to set up a courier service between his residences in Innsbruck and Brussels in 1490, their meteoric rise and prosperity in the empire began. The network was continually extended, with postal stations established at which horses and riders could be changed, and where travellers could spend a night – to this day, inns with the name "Zur Post" bear witness to the system. As a reward for their services, in the 17th century the family were ennobled with the title "count".

Later they were made princes and recognised as the descendants of the Torriani family, whose coat of arms and name they were also allowed to bear. The word "Turm" (Torre) became Thurn, while "Tasso" was altered to Taxis. Since then, the tower and badger have appeared on the coat of arms.

Seine Durchlaucht
Fürst Albert
von Thurn und Taxis
hat im Jahre 1919 die
Fürstliche
Notstandsküche
zur Behebung der
damaligen Notlage errichtet!

In the north wing, now used to accommodate guests, monks once sat in the scriptorium and made copies of the Bible. Until the 13th century St Emmeram's, with its major monastic library, was a centre of book illumination. From here visitors move on to the particularly beautiful Gothic cloister, which has traces of its original painting and wonderful carved figures on its capitals and roof bosses. In contrast to the church, the cloister was made over to the princely family. Today St Benedict's Portal in the north-east corner connects the monastery and church. In what was once the monastery garden, Prince Maximilian Karl built a neo-Gothic chapel between 1835 and 1841. All members of the family are buried in its crypt.

A tour of the palace is rounded off by a visit to the neo-Classical *Marstall* ㉜ (stables), which consists of a wing for the horses' stables and a large indoor riding hall where coaches, sledges, palanquins and sedan chairs from the 18th and 19th centuries are exhibited. The prize exhibit is undoubtedly the 19th-century gala coach in which Prince Johannes and Princess Gloria drove through the streets of Regensburg for their wedding in 1980. In the north wing the *Fürstliche Schatzkammer* ㉝ (Princely Treasury, a branch of the Bavarian National Museum) presents outstanding items such as furniture, tableware, clocks and silver gems from leading European craft workshops, reflecting the splendour of the courtly world of the high aristocracy.

Marstallmuseum
◆ *Mon-Fri 11am-5pm (April-8 Nov),*
Sat-Sun 10am-5pm (April-Dec),
www.thurnundtaxis.de

Fürstliche Schatzkammer
◆ *Mon-Fri 11am-5pm*
(April-8 Nov),
Sat-Sun 10am-5pm,
www.bayerisches-
nationalmuseum.de

Marstall

Fürstliche Schatz-kammer

Information an der Kasse

Schlosscafé

April – Oktober täglich geöffnet 10 – 18 Uhr

Tomatensuppe

Schweizer Toast

Zwiebelkuchen

Have a break

After all this religious and aristocratic ostentation, you deserve a break among the plants in the **museum café**. ◆ *10am-6pm (mid-March to mid-Nov),* www.museums-cafe.de

THE MOVE TO REGENSBURG

In 1748 Emperor Franz I, who needed an imperial representative at the Perpetual Diet in Regensburg, appointed Prince Alexander Ferdinand as his principal commissar – a political office that the princes of Thurn und Taxis held until 1806. The position was highly prestigious and entailed great costs, as the prince had to keep court like the emperor, but was obliged to meet the expenses himself. For the family this meant giving up their palace in the city of Frankfurt and moving to Regensburg. Today this dynasty is the biggest private owner of land and forest in Germany, as the Thurn und Taxis family continually acquired land, industrial companies and breweries from the proceeds of its entrepreneurial activities and compensation for the loss of its right to run the postal service. The head of the family is Albert II von Thurn und Taxis, born in 1983, for whom Princess Gloria successfully managed business affairs from 1990 to 2001 after the death of her husband Johannes.

3 TIP Finally, you are rewarded for this walk with a view of the jumbled pattern of city roofs. From the tower of the early Baroque *Dreieinigkeitskirche* (Trinity Church) ㊱, one of the first Protestant churches to be built in Bavaria, a wonderful 360-degree panorama is revealed – ideally in the afternoon, when the west façade of the cathedral glows in the sun's rays. If you have a little time, pay a visit to the church graveyard, where Baroque epitaphs show that many Protestant delegates to the Perpetual Diet were laid to rest.

Am Ölberg 1 ◆ Tue-Sun 12 noon-6pm (April-Oct)

● "SCOTTISH" CHURCH OF ST. JAKOB ㉞: Walk through *Dörnberg-Park* ㉟ to visit a Romanesque church whose north doorway still puzzles researchers. The name "Schottenkirche" derives from the Scoti, as Irish monks were called because their homeland was known as Scoti Maior (Ireland). In about 1090 such monks founded the first monastery here. The late 12th-century basilica that now stands here passed to "Scottish" Benedictines in 1515.

One of the most important monuments of German Romanesque architecture is the Schottenportal, "Scottish doorway", 15 metres wide and 8 metres high. Its 154 figures were once all painted, some of them also gilded or silvered, and the holes were filled with precious stones. The iconographic programme of the three-storey wall is still a matter of debate. The only certain point seems to be that this cycle represents the Last Judgement, heaven and hell.

Jakobstrasse 3 ◆ 9am-6pm
www.schottenkirche.de

Have a break

Just round the corner **Café Anna** has tables outside on Gutenbergplatz and serves delicious coffee, home-baked bread and cake.
Gesandtenstrasse 5 ◆ Mon-Sat 9am-7pm, Sun 9.30am-7pm, www.anna-cafe.de

Strolling and Shopping

A City Stroll

Regensburg in the Evening

Walhalla

Historical Museum

St. Emmeram

3 Days In

Strolling and Shopping

EXPULSION OF THE JEWS

The economic decline of Regensburg during the 15th century was followed by a moral low point in 1519: on 21 February the city council declared that all Jews had to leave their quarter within five days and clear out the synagogue within 24 hours. As in all other parts of Germany, in the previous decades accusations of poisoning and ritual murder of Christian children had stirred up anti-Jewish feeling in Regensburg and led to increasing restrictions of their rights. When Emperor Maximilian I died on 12 January 1519, the people of Regensburg took advantage of the interregnum to expel the Jews, who up to that time had been living around Neupfarrplatz. The entire Jewish quarter, including the synagogue and school, were destroyed, the cemetery defiled, and the grave stones built into the walls of houses as trophies.

STROLLING AND SHOPPING – IN THE OLD TOWN

Even though you have walked through the Old Town when seeing the sights, it is worth taking some time for leisurely window shopping: the Old Town of Regensburg offers something different from the mainstream retail scene of most city centres.

Shopping in the Old Town is fun twice over: strolling through the little streets and alleys and across the squares between Bismarckplatz and the cathedral, the Stone Bridge and Gesandtenstrasse, you will see beautiful things in historic surroundings. Many of the more than 500 shops are houses in patrician dwellings and consciously present their products in the ambience of an ancient building, whether in a former domestic chapel or beneath pointed Gothic arches. Furthermore, you will not find the standard mix of well-known chains and department stores, as most shops are small boutiques and owner-run specialists, mingled with countless cafés, inns, bars and pubs. The wares are a colourful combination of

exclusive brands, hip styles, regional arts & crafts and fine design, which makes a walk around the shopping district something special.

Cross the Stone Bridge to reach the picturesque Stadtamhof district, where more owner-run retail establishments are found. Many visitors like this area for its mix of pleasant cafés and specialist shops selling crafts.

3 TIP **ENCOUNTERS BETWEEN RELIGIONS**
A favourite rendezvous in the Old Town is *Neupfarrplatz*, the site of the Neupfarrkirche, the city's first Protestant church. When the weather is good, people sit here and children play in a place that is special: on this spot, where once the Jewish synagogue stood, the Israeli artist Dani Karavan has created an artwork in the shape of a flat relief on the ground ㊳, thus integrating this historic religious site into the city as a place for intercultural encounters.

It is also worth making a detour to the *market hall* right next to the Historisches Museum on Dachauplatz. To gourmets this modern glass building with its varied range of food seems like a miniature version of the famous Viktualienmarkt in Munich. And at Paul's Boutique, a café and wine bar in classic Italian style, and the Casa della Pasta you can enjoy a delicious meal.

Dachauplatz ◆ Mon-Sat 10am-7.30pm
www.markthalle-regensburg.de

If you also like to look round a shopping mall, you will be content in Regensburg. Close to the Old Town, behind the train station and connected to it via a pedestrian bridge, are the *Regensburg Arcaden*. In 95 shops on two levels you will find clothing, jewellery, electronics goods, books and everything needed for day-to-day life.

Friedenstrasse 23, ◆ 9.30am-8pm
www.regensburg-arcaden.de

DOCUMENT NEUPFARRPLATZ ③⑦

Anyone interested in Regensburg's history should go underground north of the Neupfarrkirche church: six metres beneath the surface lie the remains of the residence of a high-ranking Roman officer on the via principalis of the Castra Regina legionary camp, and traces of the Jewish quarter that existed here until the late 15th century. A multimedia presentation recounts the history of Neupfarrplatz and shows a reconstruction of part of the Jewish quarter.

Open for guided tours: ◆Thu-Sat 2.30pm, in July and August also Sun-Mon 2.30pm; buy tickets from Tabak Götz, Neupfarrplatz 3, www.regensburg.de/kultur/museen-in-regensburg/staedtische-museen/document-neupfarrplatz

The biggest shopping centre in the region is the *Donau Einkaufzentrum* north of the Danube in the district of Weichs, with 140 specialist stores and many services.

Weichser Weg 5
◆ 9.30am-8pm
www.donaueinkaufs
zentrum.de

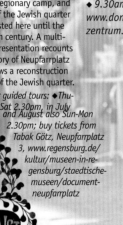

The Historical Museum

Beneath the parasols on the lawn of the Gothic cloister, the idyllic **museum café** is a wonderful place to muse on what you have seen in the exhibitions.

Tel. 0941/5676276
◆ *Mon-Fri 9am-5pm,*
Sat-Sun 9am-7pm,
www.cafe-im-museum.de

HISTORY, ART AND CULTURE – THE HISTORICAL MUSEUM ㊴

On a visit to the Historical Museum you can learn a lot of fascinating things about the history of Regensburg and eastern Bavaria. The exhibits are presented in the wonderful setting of a former Franciscan monastery.

Begin a circuit of the exhibitions on the ground floor with the model of the city, a fantastic view of how Regensburg looked in the period around 1700. Archaeological finds from prehistoric and early historic times, as well as works of art, tombstones, coins and items of everyday use from Roman Regensburg provide many impressions of the early period in the city's history. The inscription from the gate of the legionary camp can also be seen here. It shows that the Castra Regina was founded in AD 179 by Emperor Marcus Aurelius (➤ p. 46). A model illustrates the construction of the Porta Praetoria using cranes.

Continue from here to the Gothic basilica of St Salvator, the church of the Franciscan monastery. It was built in the 13th century and extended by the addition of the late Gothic choir. From 1221 the Franciscans, known as the 'ordo fratrum minorum' or Minor Friars, were established in Regensburg. Thanks to their strict observance of the ideal of poverty and their selfless dedication to pastoral work, they were equally beloved among princes and the people. They received many donations that enabled them to build their monastery. When monastic life came to an end through the dissolution of monasteries, the church was used for various purposes until it became part of the Historical Museum in 1931. Today the items on display in

the interior of the basilica, brightly lit by tall traceried windows, include many funeral monuments, among them a memorial to Berthold von Regensburg (1210-72), a famous Franciscan and preacher who spoke out clearly against persecution of the Jews.

There could hardly be a more impressive setting for an exhibition on medieval times than the rooms of the Franciscan monastery and its cloister. In addition to sculptures from the cathedral and the monastery itself, well-conceived information panels and exhibits illuminate life in the Middle Ages, the standards of living in the city, the importance of the guilds for economic activity, the disposal of waste, the meaning of sickness and death, and many more themes.

Altarpieces, panel paintings, tapestries, sculptures and other works of art complement the collection on the first and second floors, taking the story forward from the Middle Ages to the historical styles of the 19th century. There are impressive paintings by the Danube School, a movement in the art of Bavaria and northern Austria during the transition from the late Gothic to the Renaissance period. A new sensitivity to nature characterised this school, which depicted the natural world as important in its own right for the first time. One of its main exponents was from Regensburg: the engraver and painter Albrecht Altdorfer (c. 1480-1538), whose house at the corner of Obere Bachgasse (no. 7) and Augustinergasse is still standing. Work by Altdorfer that

can be seen here, for example, the remains of frescoes for the bath house in the bishop's private apartments, includes surprises such as a suggestive bathing scene in which an older man approaches a naked young woman.

LEERER BEUTEL ㊵

Around the corner from the Historical Museum stands a remarkable building, 54 metres long with seven storeys. It was once a grain warehouse, erected by the Free Imperial City in 1597 to ensure an adequate supply of grain to its citizens even in times of war or blockades by the dukes of Bavaria. Its unusual name (Leerer Beutel means "empty bag") is probably derived from Laerenpaetel, meaning "sack of grain". Today it is an arts centre, accommodating the *Städtische Galerie*, a branch of the Bavarian state collections of painting that presents 20th-century painting, sculpture, graphic art and arts & crafts from eastern Bavaria. In addition to this, a restaurant on the ground floor (➤ p. 56), the Regensburg *jazz club* (➤ p. 62) and *Filmgalerie* (➤ p. 63) are located here.

Bertoldstrasse 9
◆ Tue-Sun 10am-4pm,
www.regensburg.de/kultur/
museen-in-regensburg/
staedtische-museen/
leerer-beutel

Dachauplatz 2–4
◆ Tel. 0941/5072448, Tue-Sun 10am-4pm
www.regensburg.de/kultur/museen-in-regensburg/
staedtische-museen/historisches-museum

HOW IT ALL BEGAN

No other city in Germany can prove its age with an original founding inscription. After the destruction of the military base in today's suburb of Kumpfmühl during a war against Germanic tribes, in AD 179 the Roman Emperor Marcus Aurelius, according to an inscription on the camp gate, now in the Historical Museum, had a fortified camp measuring approximately 450 x 540 metres built at the northernmost point of the Danube, on the border between his empire and the Germanic peoples. His Castra Regina became the military centre of the whole province of Raetia. This camp or "Burg (castle) on the river Regen" later became Regensburg!

Walhalla

A BOAT TRIP ON THE DANUBE

For an enjoyable full-day outing, take a trip to *Kelheim* to visit the famous *Befreiungshalle* (Hall of Liberation), one of the great German national monuments from the 19th century. King Ludwig I commissioned construction of this circular temple to propagate the unity of the states of Germany, and had it adorned with 18 colossal statues to represent German tribes and regions. For an impressive natural spectacle, continue the journey through the *Donaudurchbruch*, the point where the river breaks through cliffs, to *Kloster Weltenburg*. Here, in the oldest Bavarian monastery, you can admire the abbey church, a complete Baroque work of art by the Adam brothers, and sample beer brewed on site in the monastery tavern.

THROUGH THE DANUBE VALLEY – WALHALLA

One of the loveliest excursions in this region is a boat trip through the romantic Danube valley to the Hall of Fame that rises above the river, 10 kilometres outside Regensburg.

ALONG THE DANUBE

From the pier next to the Historische Wurstkuchl ㊶, the boats go downriver for a distance of about ten kilometres. The first thing that catches the eye is a large construction site on the right bank: here, for the 100th anniversary of the Free State of Bavaria, the *Museum of Bavarian History* (➤ p. 65) is to open in 2018. A little further on, the next conspicuous building is a magnificent neo-Gothic structure: King Maximilian II of Bavaria had the *Königliche Villa* built in a park in the mid-19th century as a summer residence. At that time the view across country to his Walhalla was not obscured by buildings. Today this Royal Villa is a branch of the Bavarian monument conservation office. After passing the city beach with its basket chairs and loungers in front of the old warehouse, you reach the port, *Bayernhafen Regensburg*, an important logistical base and the biggest harbour in Bavaria based on the tonnage loaded and unloaded here.

For an impression of how attractive a holiday on the Danube can be, look over to the district of *Schwabelweis* on the left bank, where a large flight of steps, a sunbathing lawn and a pebble beach are an inviting spot to relax. The journey continues through the beautiful Danube valley past *Donaustauf*, where the wooden Chinese Tower in the gardens is the sole surviving part of a palace of the princes of Thurn und Taxis.

WALHALLA

From a distance you already get a glimpse of Walhalla with its majestic outdoor stairway. Framed by the outlying hills of the Bavarian Forest, it rises above the landscape on the 405-metre-high Bräuberg in the shape of a Greek temple.

This remarkable edifice was commissioned by King Ludwig I of Bavaria (reigned 1825-48), who conceived the idea of a building to forge the unity of the German people while he was still crown prince. As the country was divided into many small states following the Napoleonic Wars and the end of the Holy Roman Empire, he wished to strengthen the national identity of the Germans by means of a hall of fame: "All Germans, of whatever tribe, should always feel that they have a common Fatherland." He chose a site close to Regensburg, the city of kings and emperors. His temple of fame was named after *Walhall*, the place where fallen warriors rested in Germanic mythology.

Ludwig commissioned Leo von Klenze, one of the leading neo-Classical architects of the 19th century, to build Walhalla. Von Klenze took inspiration from the Parthenon on the Acropolis in Athens, and selected light-coloured

3 TIP If you'd rather avoid the steep, 15-minute ascent, there are several alternatives: either arrive by car, or take a taxi up to Walhalla (from the Old Town this costs about 30 euros) and return by boat, or book a Segway tour, reaching Walhalla by boat and going back to Regensburg on the Danube bike path by Segway.
www.seg-tour-regensburg.de

limestone from Kelheim as his material. After ten years of construction costing four million gulden, Walhalla was inaugurated in 1842.

After climbing the 358 steps of the stairway, visitors enter the broad interior, which is magnificently adorned with marble in various colours. On the walls are busts and plaques commemorating rulers, military leaders, scientists and artists who were regarded as role models in the 19th century, among them kings and emperors, writers such as Lessing, Schiller and Goethe, composers including Beethoven and Schubert, and painters such as Dürer and Holbein. The frieze of figures above is an idealised depiction of the history of the German peoples, from the first migrants to their conversion to Christianity in the early Middle Ages. Today new busts are still added, though not until at least 20 years

after the death of the person who is honoured. The choices are made by the ministerial council of Bavaria on the recommendations of the Bavarian Academy of Science. A total of 130 marble busts and 65 memorial plaques are now displayed.

Walhallastrasse 48
93093 Donaustauf
◆ *9am-5.45pm (April-Oct),*
9.15am-3.45pm (Nov-March)
www.walhalla-regensburg.de

Regensburger Personen-Schifffahrt Klinger GmbH, schifffahrtklinger.de

Donauschiffahrt Wurm+Köck, www.donauschiffahrt.de

Accommodation, Going Out, Tips and Adresses

Hotels

SLEEPING BEAUTY AWAKES

In the early 19th century Regensburg had fallen into a slumber that lasted over 250 years, but today the region is one of the leading economic powerhouses of Germany, thanks to a dense network of companies, research institutions and universities. The upturn began with the foundation of the university in 1967 and the establishment of new, forward-looking companies like Siemens and BMW. The university campus, home to the university, university clinic, the regional clinic and the technical high school founded in 1971, now has 33,000 students. The oldest institution of higher education, however, is the college of Catholic Church Music and Music Teaching, the world's first Roman Catholic music school when it was founded in 1874.

LOW BUDGET

● **ABOTEL HOTEL REGENSBURG**★★
Donaustaufer Strasse 70 (Reinhausen)
Tel. 0941/64090585
▲ Donaustaufer Strasse
www.abotel-regensburg.de

Low-cost accommodation in hostel dorms, about 15 minutes' walk from the Old Town.

● **BROOK LANE HOSTEL REGENSBURG**
Obere Bachgasse 21 (Old Town)
Tel. 0941/6965521
▲ Ernst-Reuter-Platz
www.hostel-regensburg.de

A hostel for young and old at the heart of the Old Town.

SUPERIOR

● **ALTSTADTHOTEL ARCH**★★★★
Haidplatz 4 (Old Town)
Tel. 0941/58660
▲ Haidplatz
www.regensburghotel.de

A four-star hotel in one of Regensburg's finest patrician houses, right on Haidplatz.

● **BISCHOFSHOF AM DOM**
Krauterermarkt 3 (Old Town)
Tel. 0941/58460
▲ Thundorfer Strasse
www.hotel-bischofshof.de

Traditional inn with individually furnished rooms and suites next to the cathedral.

● **HOTEL ZUM BLAUEN KREBS**★★★★
Krebsgasse 6 (Old Town)
Tel. 0941/57370
▲ Haidplatz
www.dicker-mann.de

Historic hotel from the 14th century in a little side street off Haidplatz, entered through a small, romantic courtyard.

● **HOTEL BOHEMIAN**★★★★
Gesandtenstrasse 12 (Old Town)
Tel. 0941/2807460
▲ Hauptbahnhof
www.bohemian-hotel.de

A small and high-class hotel, the rooms individually furnished and fitted with modern technology, with a hip bar!

● **HOTEL GOLIATH
AM DOM******
Goliathstrasse 10 (Old Town)
Tel. 0941/2000900
▲ Thundorfer-Strasse
www.hotel-goliath.de

Centrally located, modern
hotel with sauna and steam
bath.

● **HOTEL JAKOB*****
Jakobstrasse 14 (Old Town)
Tel: 0941/6009290
▲ Altes Rathaus
*www.hotel-jakob-
regensburg.de*

Hotel with modern fittings
in an 18th-century building
in the Old Town.

● **HOTEL ORPHEÉ******
Untere Bachgasse 8
(Old Town)
Tel. 0941/596020
▲ Altes Rathaus
hotel-orphee.de

Hotel in a Baroque town-
house with antique floor-
boards, Baroque doorcases
and a lovely plaster
ceiling.

● **HOTEL-ROTER-HAHN*****
Rote-Hahnen-Gasse 10
(Old Town)
Tel. 0941/595090
▲ Haidplatz
*www.roter-hahn.
com*

Cosy accommodation
in a restored 13th-
century building.

● **SORAT INSEL-HOTEL
REGENSBURG******
Müllerstrasse 7
(Oberer Wöhrd)
Tel. 0941/81040
▲ Altes Rathaus
www.sorat-hotels.com

Design hotel in Art Deco
style. The building, with a
view of the cathedral and
Old Town, used to be a factory for arts and crafts.

● **DOMRESIDENZ
HOTEL******
Tändlergasse 6 (Old Town)
Tel. 0941/37806430
▲ Domplatz
www.domresidenz.de

Apartment hotel with three
suites, furnished in an ex-
citing mix of antiques and
classics of modern design.

**BIOPARK
REGENSBURG GMBH**

Established in 1999 on
the university campus as a
company owned by the City
of Regensburg, the BioPark
is now a leading centre of
innovation that promotes
biotechnology, life sciences
and the health-related
economy in the region. The
success of this technology
and start-up centre is
demonstrated by the 37
companies that have since
then been founded in the
BioPark and by the number
of employees, which has in-
creased sixfold. At present
36 firms with 600 emplo-
yees work on the 18,000
square metres of laboratory,
office and warehouse space
of the BioPark. Promotion
of IT business and IT start-
ups is the task of R-Tech
GmbH, which has opened
a new technology centre
called TechBase, directly
next to the university and
technical high school.

*www.biopark-regensburg.de,
www.techbase.de*

Cafés

THE REGENSBURG "MUSHROOM"

It is unusual to come across a toadstool in the centre of a city – and at this one you can drink coffee. This stand-up café dates from

the 1950s. Back then, a company called Waldner from the Allgäu region invented the "Milchschwammerl" ("dairy mushroom"), a kiosk for selling milk and dairy products. 49 of them were made. Today only four remain, one of them run by Gerhard Probst in the shade of ancient trees on Fürst-Carl-Anselm-Allee. This cult café is now a protected monument.

Albertstraße 14 (Old Town)
▲ *Hauptbahnhof*
◆ *Mon-Fri 9am-7pm,*
Sun 9am-7pm,
www.facebook.com/
Regensburger-Schwammerl-
Stehcafé-im-Milchpilz

● **AAMU CAFÉ**
Thundorferstrasse 10
(Old Town)
Tel. 0176/83774862
▲ Domplatz
◆ Mo 13-19 Uhr,
Di-Fr 10-21 Uhr,
Sa-So 9.30-21 Uhr
aamu-eiscafe.de

In this Italian café they serve delicious home-made ice cream. The coffee, breakfast, paninis, pastries and snacks are equally good.

● ANNA CAFÉ REGENSBURG
Gesandtenstrasse 5
(Old Town)
Tel. 0941/2060230
▲ Haidplatz
◆ Mon-Sat 9am-7pm,
Sun 9.30am-7pm
anna-cafe.de

"ANNA loves bread and coffee". If that is not enough for you, try the freshly baked cakes or the ice cream.

● **BLACK BEAN**
Gesandtenstrasse 3–5
(Old Town)
Tel. 0941/2060631
▲ Haidplatz
◆ Mon-Fri 7.30am-9pm,
Sat 9am-11pm,
Sun 10am-8pm
black-bean.de

A pleasant coffee arcade in the historic walls of the snuff factory.

● **CAFÉ LILA**
Rote-Hahnen-Gasse 2
(Old Town)
Tel. 0941/55552
▲ Haidplatz
◆ Mon-Thu, Sun 8am-1am,
Fri-Sat 8am-2am
cafe-lila.de

From an early-morning coffee to a last cocktail, you can spend the whole day here.

● **CAFÉ RINALDI**
Alter Kornmarkt 3 a
(Old Town)
Tel. 0941/5993957
▲ Domplatz
◆ Mon-Thu 8am-10.30pm,
Fri-Sat 8am-midnight,
Sun 8am-6pm
caffe-rinaldi.de

An Italian serving a wonderful breakfast and much more.

● KAFFEELOTTE
Untere Bachgasse 5
(Old Town)
Tel. 0941/63087501
▲ Altes Rathaus
◆ Mon-Sun 10am-9pm
facebook.com/Kaffeelotte

A small and cosy café, where reading matter is provided to go with the delicious cake and chocolate.

● KAMINSKI CAFÉ
Hinter der Grieb 6
(Old Town)
Tel. 0941/5999033
▲ Altes Rathaus
◆ Mon-Thu 8am-1am, Fri-Sat 8am-2am,
Sun 9am-1am

This café with a colourful mix of customers is hidden in a side alley. The breakfast is recommended.

● KUCHENBAR
Am Protzenweiher 1
(Stadtamhof)
Tel. 0941/38216995

▲ Steinweg
◆ Wed-Fri 8am-6pm,
Sat-Sun 9am-7pm
kuchenbar-regensburg.de

Cross the bridge to try the excellent cake.

● MOCCABAR
Brückstrasse 5
(Old Town)
Tel. 0941/5865527
▲ Altes Rathaus
◆ Mon-Sun 8am-1am
moccabar-regensburg.com

A cosy café with excellent varieties of coffee and drinking chocolate.

● MORITZ CAFÉBAR
Untere Bachgasse 15
(Old Town)
Tel. 0941/5998840
▲ Altes Rathaus
◆ Mon-Sat 7.30am-1am,
Sun 9am-1am
cafemoritz.com

A café bar where you will feel at home at any time of day.

OSTENTOR

A particularly beautiful city gate, the only one in Regensburg that is completely intact, stands at the end of Ostengasse. To this day, many vehicles and pedestrians still pass through the five-storey tower, flanked by two smaller, octagonal turrets, on a daily basis.

This city gate was built in the early 14th century, when the eastern suburb was incorporated into the fortified area. To the outside, the gate presents an appearance of military strength with many arrow slits and openings for pouring boiling oil, while the side facing the city is more open, with traceried windows one above the other.

Restaurants

● BISTRO ROSARIUM
Hoppestrasse 3 A
(Westenviertel)
Tel. 0941/26885
▲ Justizgebäude
◆ Mon-Sun from 10am
bistro-rosarium.de

Specialities from Alsace
are served in the middle of
Dörnberg Park.

● BEIM DAMPFNUDEL ULI
Am Watmarkt 4 (Old Town)
Tel. 0941/53297 (keine Re-
servierungen möglich)
▲ Altes Rathaus
◆ Wed-Fri 10am-5pm,
Sat 10am-3pm
dampfnudel-uli.de

A dampfnudel is a yeast
dumpling, a Bavarian
speciality, served here by
Uli, a true Regensburg
character.

● GASTHOF-RESTAURANT DICKER MANN
Krebsgasse 6 (Old Town)
Tel. 0941/57370
▲ Haidplatz
◆ Mon-Sun 9am-1am
www.dicker-mann.de

Generally said to be the
best place for roast pork!

● KREUTZERS RESTAURANT
Prinz-Ludwig-Strasse 15 a
(Ostenviertel)
Tel. 0941/569565020
▲ Prinz-Ludwig-Strasse
◆ Mon-Fri 11.30am-2pm
and from 6pm, Sat from 6pm
kreutzers-restaurant.de

For beef or fish from a char-
coal grill, this restaurant in
the historic warehouses in
the old harbour quarter is
highly popular.

● RESTAURANT "LEERER BEUTEL"
Bertoldstrasse 9
Tel. 0941/58997
▲ Dachauplatz
◆ Mon 6pm-1am, Tue-Sat
11am-1am, Sun 11am-3pm
leerer-beutel.de

An elegant restaurant off
the tourist track in the
Städtische Galerie, where
regional dishes are served
according to the principles
of the slow food movement.

● RESTAURANT ORPHEÉ
Wahlenstrasse 1 (Old Town)
Tel. 0941/52977
▲ Altes Rathaus
◆ Mon-Sun 8am-1am
*hotel-orphee.de/
restaurant/*

Orphée has cult status for
its French cuisine in the
atmosphere of a Parisian
bistro, open from morning
to night.

● OSTERIA LUNA ROSSA
Fischgässel 1 (Old Town)
Tel. 0941/5997933
▲ Altes Rathaus
◆ Mon-Sat 5.30pm-12.30am
luna-rossa-regensburg.de

Italian meals at the heart of
the Old Town, with tables in
the romantic courtyard.

● RESTAURANT BRAND-NER
Müllerstrasse 7
(Stadtamhof)
Tel. 0941/8104470
▲ Haidplatz
◆ Tue-Sat 11.30am-midnight
*sorat-hotels.com/de/hotel/
regensburg/restaurant-
brandner.html*

Come here to get a fine view of the Danube and enjoy creative cooking.

● **AKADEMIESALON**
Andreasstrasse 28 (Stadtamhof)
Tel. 0941/46524897
▲ Haidplatz
◆ Mon-Sun from 11am
akademiesalon.de

After watching a film or going to a play or concert, you can have a wonderful Italian meal here in the Andreasstadel.

● **STORSTAD RESTAURANT**
Watmarkt 5 (Old Town)
Tel. 0941/59993000
▲ Bismarckplatz
◆ Tue-Sat 12 noon-2pm & 6-10.30pm
storstad.de

A Michelin-starred restaurant with Asian-German fusion cooking by Anton Schmaus, above the roofs of the Old Town.

REGENSBURG SPECIALITIES

Blaukraut
red cabbage

Böfflamott
braised beef

Brezn
pretzels

Erdäpfel
potatoes

Fleischpflanzerl
meat balls

Germknödel
yeast dumpling

Hendl
grilled chicken

Krautwickel
roulade wrapped in cabbage leaf

Obatzda
a Bavarian cheese speciality made from Camembert, paprika and onions

Powidl
plum sauce

Radi
white radish

Radler
shandy (beer and lemonade)

Reherl
chanterelle mushrooms

Reiberdatschi
potato cakes

Schwammerl
mushrooms

Semmeln
bread rolls

Starkbier
strong beer

Topfenstrudel
strudel with curds

Weissbier
wheat beer

Zwetschgendatschi
plum pie

Pubs & Beer Gardens

● **0941 BEACH**
Donaulände 21
(Ostenviertel)
Tel. 0176/67823298
▲ Weissenburgstrasse
◆ Sun–Thu 11am-11pm,
Fr-Sat 11am-midnight
(summer)
facebook.com/0941BEACH

Sand, loungers and a pool create a holiday atmosphere. Cool drinks and treats from the barbecue add to the enjoyment.

● **ALTE LINDE**
Müllerstrasse 1
Tel. 0941/88080
▲ Oberer Whörd
◆ 11am-11pm (Apr-Oct),
Mon-Fri 3-11pm, Sat-Sun
11am-11pm (Nov-March)
www.altelinde-regensburg.de

A beer garden with traditional Bavarian food and probably the finest view of the Old Town.

● **CAFE UNTER DEN LINDEN**
Dr.-Johann-Maier-Strasse 1
(Westenviertel)
Tel. 0941/26196
▲ Ostdeutsche Galerie
◆ 10am-midnight
cafeunterdenlinden.de

An old-established inn with a lovely beer garden in the Stadtpark.

● **DIE OMA IN DA ANTN (OMA PLÜSCH)**
Badstrasse 32 (Stadtamhof)
Tel. 0941/20909400
▲ Haidplatz
◆ Mon–Fri from 5pm,
Sat from 11.30am,
Sun 11.30am-2pm
oma-plüsch.de

Once a student pub, now the Oma (grandmother) has moved to a large beer garden right by the river Danube.

● **BRAUEREIGASTSTÄTTE KNEITINGER**
Arnulfsplatz 3 (Altstadt)
Tel. 0941/52455
▲ Arnulfsplatz
◆ 9am-midnight
www.kneitinger.de

The founding site of a traditional brewery, serving Bavarian specialities.

● **BRAUEREIGASTSTÄTTE SPITALGARTEN**
St.-Katharinen-Platz 1
(Stadtamhof)
Tel. 0941/84774
▲ Haidplatz
◆ Mon-Sun 10am-11pm
garten.spital.de

In the tavern or the large beer garden you can enjoy hearty Bavarian food with beer brewed on site.

● **HACKER-PSCHORR WIRTSHAUS**
Neupfarrplatz 15 (Altstadt)
Tel. 0941/5840455
▲ Domplatz
◆ Mon-Sun 10am-11.30pm
hacker-pschorr-regensburg.de

A cosy inn in the courtyard of what was once an Augustinian monastery at the heart of the Old Town.

● **HEMINGWAY'S**
Obere Bachgasse 3–5
(Altstadt)
Tel. 0941/561506
▲ Altes Rathaus
◆ Tue-Thu 9am-1am,
Fri-Sat 9am-2am
hemingways.de

Once a chapel with a high domed vault and black marble walls, this is a wonderful place to spend an evening.

● **CAFÉ PICASSO**
Unter den Schwibbögen 1 (Altstadt)
Tel. 0941/53657
▲ Domplatz
◆ Mon-Sun 10am-2am
cafe-picasso-regensburg.de

The historic building of a former chapel, the Salvatorkapelle, this is popular with students and other guests.

● **SCHOLZ**
D.-Martin-Luther-Strasse 2 (Altstadt)
Tel. 0941/4659441
▲ Am Königshof
◆ Mon-Sat from 9am, Sun from 10am
scholz-regensburg.de

Eat, drink and party in beautiful surroundings.

● **SPITALKELLER**
Alte Nürnberger Strasse 12
(Stadtamhof)
Tel. 0941/89059170
▲ Schwandorfer Strasse
◆ Tue-Sat 4-11pm, Sun 10am-11pm
www.spitalkeller.com

A traditional inn with a small theatre and a big beer garden shaded by trees.

REGENSBURG IN FIGURES

With a population of 150,000, Regensburg is the fourth-largest city in Bavaria, capital of the Oberpfalz administrative region and seat of the diocese of Regensburg. Approximately 55 per cent of the residents are Roman Catholic, and more than 12 per cent have foreign nationality.

Regensburg lies at the northernmost point of the Danube, at the mouths of two tributaries, the Raab and Regen. The surface area of the city is 80.76 square kilometres, measuring 12.18 kilometres from north to south and 12.07 kilometres from east to west. Its highest point lies 471 metres, its lowest 337 metres above sea level.

Thanks to a successful development policy with close networking between companies, research institutions and universities, in recent years Regensburg has become one of Germany's leading centres for business. With a university und two other institutes of higher education, more than 142,000 jobs and an unemployment rate significantly below four per cent, with Bavaria's busiest inland harbour, and the presence of many global players such as BMW, Continental, GE, Infineon, Osram and Schneider Electric, as well as healthy medium-sized companies like Händlmaier and Kronos, Regensburg is regarded as an extremely dynamic city that actively works to attract business sectors of the future through such institutions as the BioPark and the TechBase technology centre.

Tourism is a further significant source of income. With almost 980,000 overnight stays, of which 23 per cent were guests from abroad, the city takes third place in the Bavarian accommodation rankings. In a comparison of 100 top sights in Germany, Regensburg occupies 24th place, ahead of attractions such as Sanssouci Palace in Potsdam and the Museum Island in Berlin.

Bars & Nightlife

VIEW FROM THE HEIGHTS

For a superb view of Regensburg, take a trip out to the heights called Winzerer Höhen. From Wirtshaus Spitalkeller at 12, Alte Nürnberger Strasse, at the foot of the Dreifaltigkeitsberg (Trinity Hill), begin the ascent to the Dreifaltigkeitskirche, a church that citizens of Stadtamhof built in 1713 in the hope of being saved from plague. The monument on Österreicherweg is a memorial to the destruction of Stadtamhof during the Napoleonic Wars. Up on the Winzerer Höhen, note the beautiful neo-Classical villa that was once the factory of a silk-spinning company with a mulberry plantation. From here, the eight-kilometre Albertus-Magnus-Weg leads along the Winzerer Höhen and up to the Adlerberg. At many points there is a wonderful view of the Old Town of Regensburg.

● **BEATS CLUB**
St.-Peters-Weg 15
(Old Town)
▲ Am Königshof
◆ Tue-Thu 11pm-3am,
Fri-Sat 11pm- 4am
0941bar.de

A stylish club in cellar vaults beneath the Petersweg car park.

● **CHIN CHIN BAR**
Gesandtenstrasse 12
(Old Town)
Tel. 0941/2807460
▲ Bismarckplatz
◆ Mon-Wed 4pm-midnight,
Thu 4pm-1am, Fri-Sat 12
noon-1am, Sun 12 noon-
midnight *chin-chin-bar.de*

"Life is too short for bad drinks" is the motto of this location for fans of high-class bars.

● **FILMBÜHNE**
Taubengässchen 2
▲ Domplatz
◆ from 8.15pm
filmbuehne.com

A club with cult status serving delicious Augustiner beer and occasionally staging live concerts.

● **FLANNIGAN'S**
Baumhackergasse 2
(Old Town)
▲ Altes Rathaus
◆ Mon-Sat 8pm-2am
*www.facebook.com/
Flannigans-Cocktailbar*

A long-established pub where partygoers meet to cool down with a last drink.

● **HAB UND GUT BAR**
Keplerstrasse 3 (Old Town)
Tel. 0941/560635
▲ Haidplatz
◆ Tue-Sat 6pm-2am
habundgutbar.de

A cocktail bar that also serves excellent food.

● **KA5PER**
Hinter der Grieb 5
(Old Town)
Tel. 0941/59579099
▲ Altes Rathaus
◆ Mon-Fri 8pm-2am,
Sat 12 noon-2am,
Sun 5pm-midnight
ka5per.de

An attractive cocktail bar in the vaults of the historic synagogue.

● **MISS MARPLE
AND STRINGER**
Bismarckplatz 4
(Old Town)
Tel. 0941/20904439
▲ Justizgebäude
◆ Mon-Sun 10am-2am
marple-and-stringer.de

A bar with music from vinyl
records at the weekend.

● **MOOD-BAR
UND LOUNGE**
Am Wiedfang 2 (Old Town)
Tel. 0151/58559894
▲ Altes Rathaus
◆ Mon and Wed 7pm-1am,
Thu-Sun, Tue 7pm-2am
mood-regensburg.de

A hip hang-out where cof-
fee drinkers, bar flies and
night owls congregate.

● **SCALA**
Gesandtenstrasse 6/
Pustetpassage (Old Town)
Tel. 0941/52293
▲ Haidplatz
◆ Wed 8pm-3am,
Thu 11pm-3am,
Fri & Sat 11pm-4am
scalaclub.de

An institution in
Regensburg's nightlife with
electro, techno, indie and
80s/90s chart music.

● **SCHILLER CLASSIC BAR**
Rote-Stern-Gasse 4
(Old Town)
Tel. 0941/56998361
▲ Ernst-Reuter-Platz
◆ Tue-Sat 8pm-2am,
Sun 8pm-midnight
facebook.com/Schiller

A cosy cocktail bar in the
heart of the Old Town!

● **SUITE 15**
St.-Peters-Weg 15
(Old Town)
Tel. 0941/20908072
▲ Am Königshof
◆ Tue & Thu 11pm-3am,
Fri-Sat 11pm-4am
suite15.de

A club in cellar vaults with
two dance floors and weekly
party series, from rock and
indie to soul and techno.

BISMARCKPLATZ

It seems like a normal,
pretty square with a splas-
hing fountain between the
municipal theatre and the
Haus der Musik in the former president's palace.

But Bismarckplatz has
a magical attraction for
Regensburgers. Everyone
seems to meet here. When
the sun shines, many peo-
ple sit on the stone steps
and around the fountain,
and in the evening there is

hardly a free space on the
Bisse, as Bismarckplatz is
affectionately called – one
more demonstration of the
fact that Regensburg is
really not all that far away
from Italy.

Culture

BENEDICT XVI

A famous person associated with Regensburg is Pope Benedict XVI. Born Joseph Ratzinger in Marktl am Inn, he studied Catholic theology and philosophy in Freising and Munich. In 1969 he moved to the newly founded University of Regensburg, where he taught dogmatics and dogma history until he was appointed archbishop of Munich in 1977. He retained close connections to Regensburg, as his older brother Georg, formerly musical director of the Domspatzen boys' choir, lived here. Following his election to the papal throne in 2005 as Benedict XVI, he visited Regensburg in 2006 and celebrated an ecumenical mass in the cathedral. In 2013 he became the first pope in 600 years to resign voluntarily.

● ALTE MÄLZEREI
Galgenbergstrasse 20
(Galgenberg)
Tel. 0941/788810
▲Haydnstrasse
alte-maelzerei.de

For concerts, satire, cabaret, drama, readings or contemporary dance, this arts centre stages a wide range of cultural activities.

● IMPRO THEATER CHAMÄLEON
Alte Mälzerei
Galgenbergstrasse 20
(Galgenberg)
Tel. 0941/5988063
▲ Haydnstrasse
impro-theater-chamaeleon.de

The Chamäleon ensemble perform improvised drama in the STATT-Theater and the Alte Mälzerei.

● JAZZCLUB REGENSBURG E. V.
Bertoldstrasse 9
(Old Town)
Tel. 0941/563375
▲ König Strasse
jazzclub-regensburg.de

The venue for all jazz lovers: the culture and tradition of jazz are maintained here.

● **KLEINKUNSTBÜHNE STATT-THEATER**
Winklergasse 16 (Old Town)
Tel. 0941/53302
▲ Arnulfsplatz
statt-theater.de

This is Regensburg's stage for satire and cabaret.

● **REGENSBURGER BAUERNTHEATER**
Wilhelm-Raabe-Strasse 1 (Kumpfmühl)
Tel. 0941/85958
▲ Von-Richthofen-Strasse
regensburger-bauerntheater. de

Traditional Bavarian popular theatre is played here.

● **REGENSBURGER FIGURENTHEATER IM STADTPARK**
Dr.-Johann-Maier-Strasse 3 (Westenviertel)
Tel. 0941/28328
▲ Ostdeutsche Galerie
regensburgerfiguren theater.de

A puppet theatre, with a programme for both children and adults.

● **THEATER REGENSBURG**
Bismarckplatz 7 (Old Town)
Tel. 0941/5072424
▲ Justizgebäude
theater-regensburg.de

A home for five genres: musical theatre, drama, dance, youth theatre and concerts, performed at various venues.

● **THEATER IM SPITAL-KELLER**
Alte Nürnberger Strasse 12 (Stadtamhof)
Tel. 0941/6400885
▲ Steinweg
theater-im-spitalkeller.de

A stage for small-scale performances in a traditional inn.

● **REGENSBURGER TURMTHEATER**
Am Watmarkt 5 (Altstadt)
Tel. 0941/562233
▲ Altes Rathaus
regensburgerturmtheater.de

Comedy, cabaret, improvised drama and performances make up the programme at this stage above the roofs of the Old Town.

CINEMAS

● **FILMGALERIE IM LEEREN BEUTEL**
Bertoldstrasse 9 (Old Town)
Tel. 0941/2984563
▲ Ernst-Reuter-Platz
◆ Mon-Fri 10am-4pm
www.filmgalerie.de

A small theatre in a medieval grain warehouse, showing movies for cineastes and international premieres screened with subtitles.

● **KINOS IM ANDREASSTADEL**
Andreasstrasse 28 (Stadtamhof)
Tel. 0941/89799169
▲ Eiserne Brücke
kinos-im-andreasstadel.de/ index.php

An arthouse cinema

● **REGINA METROPOLIS**
Holzgartenstrasse 22 (Stadtamhof)
Tel. 0941/41625
▲ Reinhausen Brücke
reginakino.de

The top international films are shown here.

Museums

ALBRECHT ALTDORFER (C. 1480–1538)

On the corner house at Obere Bachgasse no. 15 a plaque commemorates a man who is known in art history as the main representative of the so-called Danube School and was one of the first to make landscape painting an independent genre. The painter, engraver and architect Albrecht Altdorfer, who possessed citizen's rights in Regensburg from 1505, was a respected resident of the city. As a member of the Outer Council from 1517 he was involved in the expulsion of the Jews, and made several engravings of the demolition of the synagogue. From 1527 he was a member of the Inner Council and city architect. In the latter role he remodelled the city defences. His most famous work is Alexander's Battle, commissioned by Duke Wilhelm IV of Bavaria (1528-29).

● **BRÜCKTURM-MUSEUM**
➤ S. 25

● **DOCUMENT LEGIONSLAGERMAUER**
Dr.-Martin-Luther-Strasse (Altstadt)
Tel. 0941/5071442
▲ Ernst-Reuter-Platz
regensburg.de/kultur/ museen-in-regensburg/ staedtische-museen/ document-legionslagermauer

Here are remains of buildings from Roman times.

● **DOCUMENT NEUPFARRPLATZ**
➤ S.42

● **DOCUMENT NIEDERMÜNSTER**
➤ S. 23

● **DOCUMENT REICHSTAG**
➤ S. 14

● **DOCUMENT SCHNUPFTABAKFABRIK**
Gesandtenstrasse 3/5 (Old Town)
Tel. 0941/5073442

▲ Haidplatz
◆ Fri, Sat & Sun at 2.30pm
regensburg.de/kultur/ museen-in-regensburg/ staedtische-museen/docu-ment-schnupftabakfabrik

The snuff factory, where part of the industrial history of Regensburg comes to life in the former premises of a snuff-maker.

● **DOMSCHATZMUSEUM:**
➤ S. 20

● **DONAU-SCHIFFAHRTS-MUSEUM**
Thundorferstrasse/Marc-Aurel-Ufer (Old Town)
Tel. 0941/5075888
▲ Domplatz
◆ Apr-Oct Tue-Sun 10am-5pm
regensburg.de/kultur/museen-in-regensburg/weitere-museen/donau-schiffahrts-museum

Museum of shipping history on board two historic Danube boats.

● **FÜRSTLICHE SCHATZKAMMER**
➤ S. 36

● **GOLFMUSEUM**
Tändlergasse 3 (Old Town)
Tel. 0941/51074
▲ Domplatz
◆ Mon-Sat 10am-6pm
regensburg.de/kultur/museen-in-regensburg/weitere-museen/golfmuseum

Seven centuries of golfing history, including over 1,200 rare exhibits.

● **HISTORISCHES MUSEUM**
➤ S. 44

● **KEPLER GEDÄCHTNISHAUS**
Keplerstrasse 5 (Old Town)
Tel. 0941/5073442
▲ Altes Rathaus
◆ Sat, Sun and holidays 10.30am-4pm
regensburg.de/kultur/museen-in-regensburg/staedtische-museen/kepler-gedaechtnishaus

This museum, in the house where Johannes Kepler (1571-1630) died, informs visitors about the life and work of the famous astronomer.

● **KUNSTFORUM OST-DEUTSCHE GALERIE**
Dr.-Johann-Maier-Strasse 5 (Westenviertel)
Tel. 0941/297140
▲ Ostdeutsche Galerie
◆ Tue-Sun 10am-5pm, Thu until 8pm
regensburg.de/kultur/museen-in-regensburg/weitere-museen/kunstforum-ostdeutsche-galerie

A collection of works by German artists, from the Romantic to Classical periods, from regions of eastern and south-eastern Europe that were once settled by German speakers.

● **MUSEUM IN DER DREIEINIGKEITSKIRCHE**
Am Ölberg 1 (Old Town)
▲ Haidplatz
◆ May-Sept 12 noon-6pm, Tue-Sun 12 noon-6pm
www.dreieinigkeitskirche.de

An exhibition on the history of Protestant Regensburg.

● **MUSEUM ST. ULRICH:**
➤ S. 21

● **NATURKUNDEMUSEUM OSTBAYERN**
Am Prebrunntor 4 (Old Town)
Tel. 0941/5073443
▲ Arnulfsplatz
◆ Mon 9am-12 noon, Tue-Fri 9am-4pm, Sun 10am-5pm
naturkundemuseum-regensburg.de

This museum in the Classical bishop's palace next to Herzogspark

presents the geology and the modern situation in the region of eastern Bavaria.

● **STÄDTISCHE GALERIE LEERER BEUTEL**
➤ S. 46

● **MUSEUM OF BAVARIAN HISTORY**

For the 100th anniversary of the foundation of the Free State of Bavaria in 2018, the Museum der Bayerischen Geschichte is scheduled to open on Donaumarkt next to the Eisenerzen Brücke (bridge). In contrast to other museums it will not emerge from a collection but from an idea: to present the history of the Free State of Bavaria from the point of view of its inhabitants. Bavarians were called on to contribute their personal stories and belongings to the museum. The museum is also intended to be a cultural meeting place for Bavaria, where the people from its different regions and from neighbouring regions come together.

www.museum.bayern

Shopping

HÄNDLMAIER´S SWEET MUSTARD

Regensburg's best-known export is the sweet mustard that is a must in Bavaria when eating white sausage. The recipe was created by Johanna Händlmaier, who opened a butcher's shop in Gesandtenstrasse in 1910 with her husband Karl. Four years later she came up with her recipe for sweet, home-made mustard, laying the basis for the family company that still exists. Since 1964 Händlmaier has concentrated its activities entirely on making mustard – no longer in the city centre, but on Regensburg's industrial estate in Haslbach. The company now sells a range of different mustards, various gourmet sauces and horseradish, but the main product is still, after more than 100 years, the sweet mustard.

Shop:
Untere Bachgasse
(Old Town)
Tel. 0941/58612235
▲ Altes Rathaus
◆ Mon-Sat 10am-6.30pm
www.haendlmaier.de

● BÜRSTEN ERNST MANUFAKTUR

Glockengasse 10
(Old Town)
Tel. 0941/51721
▲ Haidplatz
◆ Mon-Fri 9am-6pm,
Sat 9am-4pm
bürsten-regensburg.de/

A shop with cult status, where brushes have been made by hand and sold for four generations: brushes for vegetables, Espresso machines, animals, face massage and much more.

● CHRISTA AM KOHLENMARKT

Untere Bachgasse 1
(Old Town)
Tel. 0941/46522530
▲ Altes Rathaus
◆ Mon-Fri 10am-6pm,
Sat 10am-4pm
christaamkohlenmarkt.de

For candles, soap that looks like stone or lovely tableware, this is a place to browse.

● CORVUS WOHNITÄTEN

Goliathstrasse 8 (Old Town)
Tel. 0941/59579883
▲ Altes Rathaus
◆ Mon-Fri 10am-6pm,
Sat 10am-3pm
corvus-wohnitaeten.de

Come here to find beautiful items for the home and out-of-the-ordinary accessories.

DIBA CHOCOLAT REGENSBURG

Rote-Hahnen-Gasse 6
(Old Town)

Tel. 0941/5865864
▲ Haidplatz
◆ 10am-12pm (May-Sept.),
Mon-Sat 10am-8pm,
Sun 12am-6.30pm
(Oct.-April)
diba-chocolat.de

Delicious ice cream and fine chocolates are sold here.

● LA CASITA
Neue-Waag-Gasse 1
(Old Town)
Tel. 0941/46395857
▲ Altes Rathaus
◆ Mon-Sat 10am-6pm
regensburg.la-casita.de

A little corner shop selling interesting gifts.

● MENSCHENSKINDER
Kohlenmarkt 1 (Old Town)
Tel. 0941/59058
▲ Altes Rathaus
◆ Mon-Sat 10am-6.30pm
menschenskinder.org

A toy shop for kids of all ages.

● RETROLADEN
Wahlenstrasse 14 (Old Town)
Tel. 0941/93083003
▲ Altes Rathaus
◆ Mon-Fri 10.30am-6pm,
Sat 10am-5pm

Old design rediscovered – from vintage advertising signs to retro design and small items of furniture.

● SCHUHBECKS GEWÜRZE
Goliathstrasse 4 (Old Town)
Tel. 0941/59579601
▲ Altes Rathaus
◆ Mon-Sat 10am-7pm
schuhbeck.de/de/ geschaefte/gewuerzlaeden/ regensburg/

Spices and spice mixtures from the Michelin-starred chef Alfons Schuhbeck.

● SELMAIR
Untere Bachgasse 2
(Old Town)
Tel. 0941/51225
▲ Altes Rathaus
◆ Mon-Fri 9.30am-6.30pm,
Sat 9.30am-6pm
selmair-spielzeug.de

Here you will find something to bring back for children.

● ZINN KLEINSCHMIDT
Wahlenstrasse 4 (Old Town)
Tel. 0941/54629
▲ Altes Rathaus
◆ Mon-Fri 10am-6pm, Sat 10am-4pm, Sun 11am-4pm
zinn-kleinschmidt.de

For several generations this family company has been making beautiful things from pewter.

3 **TIP**

Hier finden Sie eine
nette Toilette
Eine Aktion von Stadt Regensburg und Stadtmarketing Regensburg

We have all encountered this problem. You are out in the city, you feel an urgent need, and no public toilet is to be found. In Regensburg the "Nette Toilette" campaign has the answer: cafés and pubs allow anyone to use their facilities without charge. Look out for a red sticker with a smiling face!

Addresses

INFORMATION

**REGENSBURG
TOURISMUS GMBH**
Wahlenstrasse 17
93047 Regensburg
Tel. 0941/5074410
tourismus.regensburg.de

TOURIST INFORMATION
Altes Rathaus
Rathausplatz 4
93047 Regensburg
Tel. 0941/5074410
◆ Mon-Fri 9am-6pm,
Sat 9am-4pm,
Sun 9.30am-4pm (Apr-Oct),
9am-2.30pm (Nov-March)
tourismus.regensburg.de

ARRIVAL/DEPARTURE

BY AIR: Regensburg can
be reached conveniently
from Nuremberg and Mu-
nich international airports:

MUNICH AIRPORT
(www.munich-airport.de) is
85 kilometres from Regensburg. There are connections
by rail or the Airportliner
service *(www.airportliner.
com*, Tel. 0941/22220). If
you hire a car, the journey
to Regensburg takes about
one hour.

The Albrecht Dürer Airport
in Nuremberg is 110 kilo-
metres from Regensburg.
The journey can be made by
rail or hire car.
www.airport-nuernberg.de

BY TRAIN: Regensburg is
reached on international
train routes: Amsterdam/
Brussels-Vienna-Budapest
and Zurich/Paris-Prague,
and with direct national
connections from Berlin/
Dresden, Hamburg/Hano-
ver, Dortmund/Cologne,
Frankfurt, Karlsruhe/Stutt-
gart and Munich.
Service hotline
0180/6 99 66 33,
www.bahn.de

The central station lies to
the south of the Old Town,
in easy walking distance.
All the important bus routes go from here, including
the Altstadtbus to the Old
Town. Taxis are at the main
exit.

Bikes: Bike-Ambulanz at
the central station hires
bicycles.
Bahnhofstrasse 18
*www.fahrradverleih-
regensburg.de* oder
Tel. 0941/5998194

BY CAR: Take highway
A3 to Regensburg from
Cologne, Frankfurt, Nu-
remberg, Passau, Vienna
and Salzburg, highway A93
from Munich, Weiden, Hof
and Dresden. Free parking
is possible on the large
car park on Wöhrdstrasse
(unsupervised). For further
information on parking, refer to *www.regensburg.de/
leben/verkehr-mobilitaet/
auto-und-motorradfahrer/
parken*.

BY OVERLAND COACH: this
is a low-cost way to get to Regensburg from other German
cities. Various operators have
services to the bus station,
which is by the train station.
www.fernbusse.de

BANKS

Banks in Regensburg open
at the usual times.
◆ 8.30am-4pm

REISEBANK REGENSBURG
Pfauengasse 1
Tel. 0941/58437861
◆ Mon 9.30am-5pm,
Tue-Fri 9am-1pm, 2-5.30pm

TICKET SALES
Mittelbayerischer
Kartenvorverkauf,
Donau-Einkaufszentrum
Weichser Weg 5
Tel. 0941/466160,
www.mittelbayerische.de

Tourist Information
Rathausplatz 1
Tel. 0941/5075050
tourismus.*regensburg.de*

HIRE CARS:
Autovermietung Wolf
Friedenstrasse 12 b
Tel. 0941/383080
www.autovermietung-wolf.de

Avis, Im Gewerbepark 38
0941/6409540
www.avis.de

Buchbinder
Margaretenstrasse 8,
Tel. 0941/51181
www.buchbinder.de

Hertz
Straubinger Strasse 75
Tel. 0941/798181
www.hertz.de

Sixt
Further Strasse 6
0180/6252525
www.sixt.de

EMERGENCY

Police	110
Fire	112
Emergency doctor	116117

Doctor: Ärztliche Bereit-
schaftspraxis Regensburg at
the hospital Krankenhaus
der Barmherzigen Brüder
Prüfeninger Strasse 86
◆ Wed, Fri 4-8pm,
Sat-Sun 8am-9pm

Emergency dentist:
Tel. 0941/5987923

Pharmacy on call:
www.aponet.de

Lost and found:
Bürgerzentrum – Fundamt,
Dr.-Martin-Luther Strasse 3,
93047 Regensburg
Tel. 0941/5075880

PUBLIC TRANSPORT

RVV Kundenzentrum
Hemauerstrasse 1
gegenüber dem Bustreff
Albertstrasse
Tel. 0941/6012888
◆ Mon-Fri 8am-6pm
www.rvv.de

POST

Post office:
Bahnhofstrasse 16,
◆ Mon-Fri 8am-6.30pm,
Sat 8am-12.30pm
Post office: Domplatz 3
◆ Mon-Fri 9.30am-6pm,
Sat 9.30am-12.30pm

CITY TOURS

Cultheca CulturEvents
Dr. Peter Styra
Werftstrasse 6
Tel. 0941/58612330
www.cultheca.de

Church tours:
Infozentrum DOMPLATZ 5
Domplatz 5
Tel. 0941/5971662
domplatz-5.de

kulttouren – Verband der Regensburger Gästeführer e. V.
Geschäftsstelle:
Seifensiedergasse 14
Tel. 0941/
507-3413/-3417
*www.
kulttouren.
de*

Regensburg Aktiv
Roland Wimmer
St.-Georgen-Platz 10
Tel. 0941/20062112

SEG TOUR GmbH
Frauenbergl 2
Tel. 0941/758612684
www.seg-tour-regensburg.de

Stadtmaus
Thundorferstrasse 1
Tel. 0941/2303600
stadtmaus.de

Tourist Information
Altes Rathaus,
Rathausplatz 4
Tel.: 0941/5074410
tourismus.regensburg.de

TAXI

Taxi Regensburg:
Tel. 0941/52052
CB Taxi Regensburg:
Tel. 0941/8905203

3 TIP The Regensburg CARD gives you free use of local public transport
for either 24 or 48 hours and discounts on admission to the Regensburg museums and cathedral, as well as on boat trips with Regensburger Personenschifffahrt Klinger, at the municipal theatre, the Kletterwald
climbing park and for city tours with KultTouren e.V. - Verband der Regensburger Gästeführer. You also have special offers in five other Bavarian holiday regions. The Regensburg CARD is available from the tourist information
office, the RVV public transport customer centre, in many hotels and from
other partners.
www.stadtmarketing-regensburg.de/projekte/regensburg-card.html

Regensburg History

About 90 AD	A Roman fort is built in the area of today's Kumpfmühl district.
179 AD	Under Emperor Marcus Aurelius a fortified legionary camp, the Castra Regina of the III Italic Legion, is established.
About 600	The Castra Regina becomes the ducal residence of the Agilolfing dynasty, and thus the first capital of Bavaria.
739	The missionary bishop Boniface establishes the diocese of Regensburg.
791	Written mention of the first imperial assembly under Charlemagne.
825–876	King Ludwig the German resides in the newly built palace.
12th and 13th century	Regensburg's golden age. It is one of the most prosperous and largest cities in the empire.
1135–1146	Construction of the Stone Bridge.
1245	Emperor Friedrich II grants rights of self-government; Regensburg becomes a Free Imperial City.
1273	Following a fire, construction of the new cathedral begins.
About 1500	Economic decline sets in.
1496	Stadtamhof becomes an independent town.
1519	Expulsion of the Jews from the city.
1542	The city council converts to Protestantism.
1663–1806	An imperial assembly, the "Perpetual Diet of Regensburg", is held.
1748	The imperial General Postmaster, Prince Alexander Ferdinand von Thurn und Taxis, is appointed as the emperor's deputy at the Reichstag.
1806	The Holy Roman Empire of the German Nation is dissolved in Regensburg.
1810	Regensburg becomes part of the Kingdom of Bavaria.

1859 Railway lines to Munich and Nuremberg are opened.

1872 Completion of the cathedral.

1924 Stadtamhof is incorporated into the city.

1945 The Danube bridges are blown up, and the city surrenders without fighting to American forces.

1967 The university is opened.

1978 The Regensburg-Kelheim section of the Rhine-Main-Danube Canal is opened.

1995 Regensburg celebrates the 750th anniversary of becoming a Free Imperial City.

1999 Foundation of the BioPark Regensburg, which becomes one of the most modern centres of biotechnology in Bavaria.

2006 The Old Town ensemble of Regensburg including Stadtamhof is declared UNESCO World Heritage.

2006 Pope Benedict XVI visits Regensburg.

2014 Two major events are held in Regensburg: the 99th German Catholic Conference and an exhibition of the state of Bavaria: "Ludwig the Bavarian. We are emperor".

2015 Inauguration of the new football stadium, the Continental Arena Regensburg.

2018 Reopening of the St Ulrich Museum and opening of the Museum of Bavarian History are scheduled.

Regensburg CARD

- › Free transport by bus and train
- › Special deals at cultural and leisure venues

Available at the tourist information centre in the old town hall (Altes Rathaus), at the world heritage visitors' centre in the Salzstadl, and in many shops around Regensburg.

Tel. +49 941 507-4410, tourismus@regensburg.de

www.regensburg-card.de